Knowing Levels and Developmental Stages

Contributions to Human Development

Vol. 16

Series Editor
John A. Meacham, Buffalo, N.Y.

Basel · München · Paris · London · New York · New Delhi · Singapore · Tokyo · Sydney

Knowing Levels and Developmental Stages

Robert L. Campbell, Yorktown Heights, N.Y.
Mark H. Bickhard, Austin, Tex.

 **KARGER**

1986

Basel · München · Paris · London · New York · New Delhi · Singapore · Tokyo · Sydney

Contributions to Human Development

National Library of Medicine, Cataloging in Publication
    Campbell, Robert L.
    Knowing levels and developmental stages/
    Robert L. Campbell, Mark H. Bickhard. – Basel; New York: Karger, 1986. –
    (Contributions to human development; vol. 16)
    Bibliography: p.
    Includes indexes.
    1. Human Development   2. Models, Psychological   I. Bickhard, Mark H.
    II. Title   III. Series
    Wl CO778S v. 16 [BF 713 C189k]
    ISBN 3-8055-4262-3

Contents

Preface

This monograph reformulates developmental stages in terms of a hierarchy of knowing levels derived from an underlying interactive model of knowing [*Bickhard*, 1978, 1980a]. It is part of an ongoing conceptual investigation of the potentialities of psychological development, and the constraints on development, that emerge from the underlying ontology of psychological processes. A preliminary treatment of developmental sequences has already appeared [*Campbell and Richie*, 1983] and an examination of developmental domains is currently in progress [*Richie*, 1984].

The knowing-level conception of developmental stages was developed over 10 years ago from the interactive model of knowledge [*Bickhard*, 1980a], independently of Piagetian approaches to stages. *Bickhard* [1978] presented the model of stages in a schematic form, and contrasted the transition from level 1 to level 2 with *Piaget's* conception of the transition to concrete operations. Although level 3, and the higher levels beyond it, were mentioned in this earlier treatment, they were not examined in detail, or contrasted with *Piaget's* conception of formal operations.

We began work on this monograph in October 1982 with the aim of contrasting knowing-level 3 with formal operations. Not only did this seem to be an appropriate next step in developing the model, it also seemed appropriate in light of the conceptual difficulties that the structural conception of formal operations was obviously having, and the proliferation of partial alternatives that were being suggested in the literature. Moreover, empirical studies of the logical necessity of class inclusion had led to perplexity about the development of necessity and the status of *Piaget's* distinction between concrete and formal operations. It was clear that the distinction between levels 2 and 3 would help to resolve this perplexity. Finally, we wanted to explicate *Piaget's* crucial, but rather shadowy and mysterious, conception of reflective abstraction, and the knowing-levels model provided an explication.

As we pursued our critique of the algebraic structures that *Piaget* had used to model formal operations, it became clear that issues were being raised about the theoretical status, and the explanatory value, of *any* structural model of cognition and development. Discussions of stages in the literature, and attempts to construct post-Piagetian stage models, all incorporated structural presuppositions. Although structures had been previously criticized from an interactive standpoint [*Bickhard*, 1980b, 1982], these foundational criticisms needed considerable elaboration. We encountered defenses of structural stage models that relied on *Chomsky's* competence – performance distinction. We found that this distinction, often considered innocuous, was itself based on the same erroneous presuppositions that underlay structural stage models. A closer examination of *Piaget's* own work on necessity and reflective abstraction showed that his attempts to explicate developmental processes were increasingly coming in conflict with his structural accounts of developmental stages. *Piaget's* structuralism was incompatible with his constructivism. All of these considerations led us to develop a general critique of structuralism and structural conceptions of developmental stages.

Another extension of the knowing-levels approach converged with the recent interest in 'postformal' development and the proliferation of stage models that incorporate postformal stages. The knowing-levels approach provides answers to a number of questions in this rapidly developing area of inquiry, such as the debate about the existence of an upper bound to stage development. Many of the postformal accomplishments now being studied can be attributed to higher levels in the strict hierarchy of knowing levels (levels 4, 5, 6, etc.). However, it has also been clear for some time that the interactive model supports dimensions of development beyond the strict knowing-levels hierarchy. For instance, explicit considerations about reflective abstraction (metareflection) do not belong to any of the knowing levels, but rather form the basis for another developmental dimension.

An extension of the knowing-levels model in a different direction arose from challenges to the generality of *Piaget's* formal operations. Although *Piaget* claimed that the structural stage model could account for adolescent personality characteristics and for the development of identity, the explicit structural model is sharply restricted to a narrow range of scientific reasoning tasks. By contrast, the knowing-levels conception should be applicable to any developmental domain. To document this claim, we briefly sketch the development of the self and identity in terms of reflective abstraction. Similarly, investigations of personality and psychotherapy and of moral development made it clear that the knowing-level approach extends to include values in general. The development of values inherently involves reflective abstraction: we propose that values are metagoals, goals about lower-level goals.

When we attempted to include all of these extensions and applications of the basic knowing-level approach, it became clear that our treatment of developmental stages had grown too large for a single article, or even a once projected series of three articles, and required a full monograph. For such a monograph, some questions *foundational* to our conception of stages needed to be discussed. One was the nature of explanations in developmental psychology: What was the role of stages in an explanatory account of development? The conception of explanation that psychologists employ governs their approach to this issue. A critique of the common practice in psychology of reifying descriptions into explanations, and of the particular version of that practice represented by Chomskyan and derivative competence-performance distinctions, results in a differentiation between description and explanation, and in a conception of explanation, that are not standard in contemporary psychology. We argue that explanation requires a multileveled theoretical ontology – an ontology of abstract process in the case of psychology – and an explicit concern about necessities and possibilities derived from that ontology. These requirements are coming to be recognized by contemporary philosophy of science. Psychology, however, continues to be dominated by logical positivism and world-view philosophies of science which do not adequately acknowledge the role of ontology in science.

The other foundational question was the basis for the hierarchy of knowing levels which we use to model stages. The hierarchy of knowing levels derives from an underlying interactive model of knowing and representation [*Bickhard*, 1980a]. We sketch the features of the interactive model most relevant to developmental processes and stages. We contrast the interactive conception of representation with the standard view of representations as encodings, and show that the encoding conception is fundamentally incoherent: it is impossible for all representations to be encodings. We discuss the constructive metaprocess of development and contrast it with learning; show how the hierarchy of knowing levels derives from two basic properties of interactive knowing; and describe the macroevolutionary sequence of knowing, learning, emotions, and consciousness.

The general form of the model of knowing levels and developmental stages that emerges from the interactive model is illustrated by the diagram on the cover. A level 1 subsystem within the overall knowing system interacts with and knows the environment – indicated by the interactive arrows between level 1 and the environment. This level 1 subsystem itself has properties which may be interactively known from a level 2 subsystem. Level 2, in turn, has properties which may be known from level 3, etc. The potentiality of properties which are implicitly present at one level of knowing becoming explicitly known from the next higher level iterates unboundedly, generating the primary knowing levels hierarchy. This hierarchy, in turn, generates the corresponding knowing levels developmental stages model: no system at a given knowing level can be constructed, can develop, unless there are already existing systems at all lower knowing levels supporting it. Development through the knowing levels, then, must proceed in a strict stage sequence. This is the central model explored throughout the book.

We are indebted to the Jean Piaget Society for providing a forum in which conceptual and philosophical arguments about development are taken seriously. Parts of Chapters 4, 5, 6, 8, and 9 were presented in preliminary versions at the Jean Piaget Society Symposium in Philadelphia, June 1983, under the title 'Knowing levels: An alternative to formal operations'. A different version of part of Chapter 4 was presented at the Jean Piaget Society in June 1984 as 'Competence and performance: An inappropriate defense of structural stages'.

This monograph is a fully collaborative undertaking. We would like to thank *David Moshman, Michael Commons, David O'Brien, Henry Markovits,* and *Michael Richie* for their comments on previous versions.

1. Introduction

In this monograph, we present a new conception of developmental stages. Standard approaches, beginning with *Piaget*, have defined stages in terms of task-descriptive structures. By contrast, we define stages in terms of a potential hierarchy of knowing levels that derives from an interactive model of knowing [*Bickhard*, 1978, 1980a]. Knowing-level stages are intrinsic constraints on development that derive from the character of constructive developmental metaprocesses; they have an explanatory force that purely descriptive structural stages cannot have.

Our monograph can be divided into three major sections. Chapters 2 and 3 present preliminary considerations about explanation in developmental psychology and the underlying interactive model of psychological processes. Chapters 4 and 5 contain our core arguments that contrast knowing-level stages with structural stages, and explicate reflective abstraction, the process of ascent through the knowing levels. Chapters 6 through 8 apply the knowing-levels approach to specific problem areas: the development of logical necessity; development beyond *Piaget's* stage of formal operations; and the development of self, identity, and values.

Our conception of stages presupposes a contrast between descriptive and explanatory theories in psychology. It also presupposes a conception of intrinsic constraints on developmental possibilities that derive from the nature of the developmental processes. These presuppositions run counter to standard metatheoretical conceptions in psychology. In Chapter 2, we sketch an account of scientific explanation in psychology from which our conception of intrinsic constraints derives. We emphasize the importance of ontological assumptions and arguments for explanatory theories, and the related importance of the power of the modeling languages in which psychological theories are stated.

Our conception of stages is based on a hierarchy of levels of knowing that arises through the reflective iteration of a basic interactive knowing relationship. In Chapter 3, we sketch the interactive model of knowing [for more extensive treatments, see *Bickhard*, 1980a, b]. We contrast the basic conception of interactive representation with the standard view of representation as encoding, and show that the encoding conception is fundamentally incoherent. The interactive conception of developmental metaprocesses is introduced, and the properties of the knowing relationship that generate the hierarchy of knowing levels are described. Interactive approaches to learning, emotions, consciousness, perception, and language are touched on briefly.

Chapter 4 presents the fundamental contrast between knowing-level stages and structural stages. General properties of knowing-level and structural stages are contrasted (generality across domains, temporal homogeneity, relevance to developmental processes, etc.). We also make specific comparisons between knowing-level 3, and its rough counterpart in *Piaget's* theory, formal operations. We address attempts to defend structural stages by invoking the Chomskyan competence – performance distinction; this distinction simply presupposes the central error of structuralism, taking descriptive theories as explanatory. We discuss the difference between hierarchies of control and hierarchies of knowing levels, and show that structural stage accounts of any type are only capable at best of modeling hierarchies of control.

Chapter 5 examines the crucial process of ascent between stages: reflective abstraction. We show how reflective abstraction can be modeled straightforwardly within the interactive model. We contrast the knowing-level approach with *Piaget's* discussions of reflective abstraction. In *Piaget's* most advanced and explicit discussion of reflective abstraction, conceptions of the process of reflective abstraction come into conflict with structural conceptions of the outcomes of the process. By contrast, non-Piagetians and anti-Piagetians have generally tried to replace reflective abstraction with 'metacognition' and 'accessing', conceptions which as usually defined do not acknowledge knowing levels or reflective consciousness, and therefore cannot do the work of reflective abstraction.

In Chapters 6 through 8, we undertake some broad applications of the knowing-levels approach, contrasting them where possible with existing structural conceptions. Chapter 6 tackles questions about the development of logical necessity. Recent research (on class inclusion, for example) has documented developmental transitions from implicit to explicit logical necessity. Such transitions are anomalous for structural stage models: they violate structural definitions of necessity, and seem to be happening in the middle of a structurally defined stage. By contrast, they are perfectly natural from the knowing-levels standpoint.

In Chapter 7, we consider development beyond formal operations, an area that has recently received much attention. We contrast the knowing-levels approach to 'postformal' stages with structural, dialectical, and personality-oriented approaches. The interactive model of knowing yields possible developmental dimensions beyond the simple hierarchy of knowing levels, and at least some of these other dimensions have actually been instantiated in human development. Reference to these additional dimensions helps to resolve the question of an upper bound on stage development, and problems of philosophicocentrism in modeling postformal stages.

In Chapter 8, we outline the knowing-levels approach to the development of self, identity, and values. We show that the knowing-levels approach can be generalized to these areas that structural models have been conspicuously unsuccessful in accounting for. We also show that the development of the self, and more deeply, the development of values, inherently involve reflective abstraction and ascent through the knowing levels. Standard approaches that lack a knowing-level hierarchy are incapable in principle of modeling values and their development.

We conclude (Chapter 9) that knowing levels are a suitable programmatic alternative to structural stage conceptions. Changes in *Piaget's* own theory, and outside critiques and partial alternatives to structural stages, especially formal operations, have been converging on the knowing-level conception for some time. However, none of these convergent approaches has produced a general critique of structuralism, or a reformulation of stages based on conceptions of developmental metaprocess. The knowing-levels approach supplies such a reformulation.

Throughout the monograph, our criticisms are primarily directed at Piagetian or post-Piagetian structural stage conceptions. However, our arguments imply a fortiori that information-processing approaches to development [e.g., *Siegler*, 1981; *Kail and Bisanz*, 1982; *Sternberg and Powell*, 1983] are inadequate, whether they posit stages or not. Information-processing theories, whose modeling languages are committed to the unviable assumption of foundationally encoded information [see *Bickhard*, 1982, and Chapter 3 below], tend, in addition, to commit the basic structuralist error of taking task descriptions as accounts of internal processes and representations. Our discussion, however, emphasizes *Piaget's* schemes, groupings, and lattices, instead of the rules, scripts, schemas, components, and other kinds of structural descriptions favored by information-processing theorists. We have emphasized *Piaget* because he attempted a consistently developmental approach to psychology, although he did not always succeed. With the exception of *Klahr* [1984], information-processing theorists show no recognition that psychological questions are inherently developmental. Moreover, *Piaget* exhibited much more conceptual daring than any information-processing theorist ever has. *Piaget* tried to answer questions about consciousness, about the development of necessity, about the nature of logical inference, about reflective abstraction; information-processing theories have not tackled these issues. *Piaget* attempted to answer the nativist arguments of *Fodor* [*Piattelli-Palmarini*, 1980] and show that genuine novelty is possible in development; information-processing theorists have not addressed *Fodor's* arguments. We are indebted to *Piaget* for asking the right kinds of questions about development.

The task of analyzing and criticizing *Piaget* is complicated by the presence of multiple themes in his thought. The relative importance of these themes changed markedly during *Piaget's* career. At all times, *Piaget* retained an underlying interest in *epistemological* questions. *Piaget's* commitment to an interactivist and consequent constructivist (see Chapter 3) approach to knowledge stemmed from this basic interest, although his interactivism, especially, was never explicated in a fully coherent manner. In the later part of *Piaget's* career [e.g., 1977a, b, 1978], his epistemological interests often focused on consciousness and epistemic reflection, issues of central importance for the knowing-level approach.

Obviously, another prominent theme in *Piaget's* [e.g., *Piaget*, 1972a; *Inhelder and Piaget*, 1958] thought was *structuralism:* the use of mathematical structures as formal descriptions, and purported explanations, of abilities at different levels of development. The account of concrete operations, in terms of groupings, and the formal model of formal operations, in terms of the combinatorial and the INRC group, were central to *Piaget's* structuralism. *Piaget* [1970a, p. 5] regarded structures as having an intrinsic, meaningful dynamic: 'the notion of a structure is comprised of three key ideas: the idea of wholeness, the idea of transformation, and the idea of self-regulation'. Although attributing such properties to structures gave them apparent explanatory force, it was incompatible with the mathematical formalisms that *Piaget* used to characterize structures. Mathematically, algebraic structures like groupings and lattices are essentially static [see Chapters 4 and 5 below]. Although *Piaget* never fully abandoned structural models, structuralism diminished steadily in importance in his work after 1965 [*Vuyk*, 1981]. As his interest in structuralism declined, *Piaget* began to turn toward a variety of *functionalism* that employed cybernetic concepts and showed affinities with artificial intelligence and information-processing approaches; this functionalism is particularly evident in his late work on equilibration [*Piaget*, 1975].

The multiple themes in *Piaget's* thought, and their changing importance over the years, make it impossible to identify a single, unified, and internally consistent 'hard core' [*Lakatos*, 1978] in Piagetian theory. Developmental psychologists, when confronted with the Piagetian legacy, have to choose which ideas are to be retained and developed, and which ideas are to be discarded. From the standpoint of the interactive model, it is *Piaget's* epistemological interactivism, with its consequent constructivism and epistemic reflection, which is the most insightful and important. We will argue that *Piaget's* fundamental concerns about epistemology are not well served by either structuralist or functionalist approaches. They are much better served by the interactive model and the knowing-levels approach that derives from it.

A theme throughout the monograph, although not the topic of any one chapter, is that *developmental metaprocesses* are, at the core, what developmental psychology is about. The lawful organization of development over time, into sequences, domains, and stages, emerges as intrinsic constraints from the character of developmental metaprocesses. What essentially changes with development is the cognitive processes on which metaprocesses operate; the task capabilities that change over time are a complex result of the changes in underlying processes, and not the primary object of developmental study.

A few theorists have recognized that developmental processes are an inherent part of developmental analysis. *Klahr* [1984] contends that 'developmental tractability' is an important consideration in evaluating accounts of developmental sequences. *Siegel* et al. [1983] argue that transition mechanisms must be included in developmental analysis. *Cooper* [1984] considers how each new step in early number development could arise through specific developmental mechanisms, and recommends this type of analysis more generally. So far, however, these arguments have not been extended to the point of recognizing that developmental process constraints are necessary to ground a temporal ordering as a genuine, lawful sequence [cf. *Campbell and Richie*, 1983]. Moreover, the prevailing view remains that development can be adequately described as a sequence of states (an ordering of performance on tasks of increasing structural complexity). The states can be described piecemeal, and sequenced using empirical ordering information; only then should questions about transition mechanisms be seriously entertained [*Wohlwill*, 1973; *Kail and Bisanz*, 1982; *Colby* et al., 1983]. If the approach taken in our monograph is anywhere near the correct one, it entails the utter inadequacy of this prevailing view.

Our monograph focuses on developmental stages, and on specific contrasts between the knowing-levels approach and structural approaches to stages. The implications of our analysis are not confined to a narrow subdiscipline of psychology, however. They are relevant to cognitive psychology in general. Cognitive psychology typically tries to build explanatory models of adult performance without explicitly admitting intrinsic developmental constraints on the plausibility or admissibility of the models. Even if this program of building context-independent, purely synchronic models of adult abilities could be sustained, our treatment of psychological explanation in Chapter 2 and our critique of encodingism in Chapter 3 would still necessitate considerable departures from standard approaches. But the interactive model, and the knowing-levels approach to stages, imply that cognitive psychology *is* developmental psychology. Any model of knowledge is subject to questions about how the processes that it posits could have developed or evolved [*Bickhard*, 1979]; conversely, conceptions about development heuristically constrain possible models of adult cognition. This insistence on a genetic perspective was a key part of *Piaget's* constructivist program, one that needs to be carried forward.

Our account of developmental stages is also relevant to education. Intrinsic constraints on development apply in all environments – to what children understand when directly taught, as well as what they acquire informally in other settings. Intrinsic constraints often permit classes of developmental pathways besides the sequence or sequences usually followed, but they do not permit just any order of acquisition. (There are many interesting and unexplored issues here, like possible differences of an entire knowing level between the prerequisites for learning something that is directly taught, or that has extensive 'scaffolding' to prepare it, and discovering it for oneself.) Moreover, the process of reflective abstraction is rarely recognized at all in approaches to education. An outstanding exception is the work of *Papert* [1980]. *Papert* and his collaborators have developed Turtle geometry as an aid to acquiring geometric concepts from the child's own procedures for moving through space. He also recommends programming in a structured language like LOGO as a way to facilitate the child's abstraction of properties of procedures by reflecting on his or her planning processes (cf. our account of reflective abstraction in Chapter 5). Unfortunately, *Papert* never refers explicitly to reflective abstraction; he obscures his insights by trying to express them in terms of Piagetian structuralism.

More broadly, our arguments have some consequences for the relationship between psychology and philosophy. The distinction between descriptive and explanatory models helps to resolve the problematic relationship between psychology and formal logic. We contend (in Chapter 4) that formal logics in principle cannot model the processes by which people solve reasoning tasks, and so cannot be adequate explanations of reasoning performance. Moreover, the existing structural models based on formal logic that we review in Chapter 4 are not adequate descriptions of possible performance on classes of reasoning tasks. In Chapter 7 we point out further that formal logics cannot adequately describe task performance at a developmental stage, because logics are based on a norm of logical consistency, and this is not the only or the most basic value criterion for an interactive knowing system. From a developmental standpoint, formal logic is a product of reflective abstraction and decontextualization from actual procedures for making inferences (see Chapters 5 and 7); such procedures are much richer than the formal systems that have so far been abstracted from them. A clear case of the difficulty of formally capturing the rich and complex character of reasoning is the difficulty that modern formal logic has had in formalizing logical implication; the intensional logic that *Piaget* [1977b] considered necessary to model signifying implication does not yet exist. From our standpoint, formal logic does not state the 'laws of thought' in some explanatory fashion, nor can it be regarded as an a priori, self-sufficient activity of manipulating symbols. The philosophical conception of the nature of logic most closely related to our own would be the neo-Aristotelian view [e.g., *Rasmussen*, 1983] that logic pertains to 'second intentions', to our means of knowing as objects of thought, rather than to 'first intentions' or instruments of thought. The distinction between first intentions as means of knowing the world, and second intentions as the product of reflection on first intentions, is parallel to our basic distinction between knowing-level 1, which knows the environment, and knowing-level 2, which knows properties of procedures at knowing-level 1.

Another issue raised by our monograph is the lack of communication between psychology and philosophy of science. Psychology has been isolated from interesting developments in philosophy of science over the last 10–15 years. *Shapere's* [1977, 1984] concerns about the nature of scientific knowledge, *Laudan's* [1977] conception of scientific research traditions that attempt to solve both conceptual and empirical problems, and the investigations into the rationality of scientific discovery by *Nickles* [1980a, b], *Shapere* [1984], and others, are all vitally important to psychology but have had no impact on the field. The ontologically based accounts of causal explanation advanced by *Harré* [1970] and *Wallace* [1974] have been used in empirical investigations of children's conceptions of physical causality [e.g., *Bullock* et al., 1982], but have not been applied to questions about psychological explanation. In psychology, world-view approaches to philosophy of science [*Kuhn*, 1962; *Lakatos*, 1978] are regarded as the new wave, and logical positivism exerts a strong vestigial influence. Severe criticisms of world-view approaches by *Laudan* [1977], *Suppe* [1977], *Shapere* [1984] and others remain unknown or unappreciated.

In the meantime, philosophers of science have paid little attention to the problems and challenges of psychology. Although *Nickles* [1980a] recognizes cognitive psychology as a necessary source for accounts of scientific reasoning and problem-solving, no connection between psychology and philosophy of science has yet developed. Contemporary philosophy of science relies on detailed case studies and histories of science as a source of information about scientists' actual concerns, patterns of reasoning, and decision criteria. Such case studies have almost invariably been drawn from the natural sciences (physics, astronomy, sometimes biology), not from psychology.

Unlike philosophers of science, philosophers of mind [e.g., *Dennett*, 1978; *Putnam*, 1980; *Block*, 1980a, b] have been concerned about psychology. Unfortunately, their narrow agenda of issues (mind-brain reduction, functionalism, Chomskyan nativism, personal identity) often fails to touch on the genuine conceptual problems in the field. Moreover, contemporary philosophy of mind, like contemporary psychology, has been isolated from recent developments in philosophy of science.

It would be beneficial to both disciplines if serious discussions between psychologists and philosophers of science could get under way. In Chapter 2, we will discuss some philosophy of science issues that are foundational for our account of developmental stages. We will be concerned with the nature of explanation in psychology, the difference between descriptive and explanatory models, the role of metaphysical assumptions in explanation, and the need for sufficiently powerful modeling languages. We will distinguish our view of explanation in developmental psychology from those that currently prevail in the field, such as Piagetian structuralism, world-view philosophies of science, and the remnants of logical positivism.

2. The Explanatory Role of Developmental Stages

Philosophy of Science

In this chapter, our purpose is to sketch a philosophy of science framework for developmental psychology. In particular, we will be concerned with the character of explanatory models in developmental psychology, and with the explanatory role of developmental stages in those models. Our framework does not pretend to be complete or synoptic. The philosophy of science is undergoing rapid development, and most of the recent work has focused on physics, astronomy, and biology, rather than the specific problems of psychology. In consequence, much work needs to be done. However, a number of recent philosophers of science [e.g., *Harré*, 1970; *Shapere*, 1977, 1984; *Laudan*, 1977] have offered accounts of scientific explanation and of the role of metaphysical considerations in science that are relevant to the problems of psychology. They have also provided valuable critiques of orientations still popular in psychology, such as logical positivism and world-view philosophies of science. We have added some conceptions of our own, concerning the difference between explanatory and descriptive models in psychology, intrinsic constraints on development, and the power of the languages in which psychological models are constructed.

It should be noted that our use of ideas from a particular philosopher of science does not imply agreement with his or her claims about psychology. Although we make use of *Harré's* [1970] conceptions about causal explanation and lawfulness as elaborated in his philosophy of natural science, we do not agree with his approach to psychology. This is a variety of hermeneuticism which denies any real constraints on development within the individual; instead, individuals are entirely subordinated to the language community in which they live [*Harré*, 1984]. (For a critique of this aspect of hermeneutics, see Chapter 8.) More generally, we reject the belief in an unbridgeable gap separating the natural sciences from psychology that prevails among some hermeneuticists; such a belief concedes natural science to the impoverished and erroneous conceptions of scientific reasoning typical of positivism.

The ontology behind our conception of psychological explanation requires elaboration from the standpoint of the interactive model of knowing (see Chapter 3). We will rely here on intuitive conceptions of particulars (entities, things), of powers of particulars (what things do), and of realism. For *Harré and Madden* [1975], particulars and their powers are part of a substance-based ontology (although their substances are not static and their concept of a 'particular' is broad enough to include fields of force as well as trees and atoms). A realistic theory is one that attempts a correct description of some kinds of particulars and their powers, rather than just accounting for observations. For the interactive approach, it is necessary to consider how entities and powers are interactively represented. Within this approach conceptions of realism involve considerations about relations of interactive implicit definition between the knowing system and the aspects of the world that are known, and the progressive differentiation of ontological categories by the knowing system (interactive representation is discussed in Chapter 3).

The Nature of Explanation

Fundamental to the question of developmental stages is what kind of explanation stages provide, or what their role in an explanatory theory might be. To address these issues, we must consider what an explanatory account of psychological processes, or of their development, should consist of. We must also show what distinguishes psychological explanations from psychological descriptions of various kinds, such as descriptions of potential task performances.

We will contend that adequate explanations of psychological processes and representations, and of their development, depend on accounts of what these processes *are*. It is necessary to take the *psychological ontology* of our theories and models seriously. We need realistic models of processes which, although unobservable, are capable of being analyzed and explored. To develop an account of stages and of reflective abstraction, it is necessary to deal with problems, like the nature of consciousness, that have 'proven particularly recalcitrant and uncomfortably metaphysical for a psychology never truly weaned from a strict radical behaviorist tradition' [*Brown* et al., 1983, p. 111]. It is also crucial to come to grips with issues of *necessity*: to consider what could be and what must be, not just what has been observed to be.

An examination of scientific explanations shows that efficient causal explanations of relations between events (the standard for positivism and textbook experimental psychology) are not the only kind of explanation, nor the most basic kind. Other types of explanations go beyond a sequence of unanalyzed events to consider the internal structure or inherent properties of the interacting entities. Such properties themselves may in turn be subject to explanation. An approach that undertakes such explanatory tasks in constructing models of psychological processes needs a rich and productive ontology, with multiple levels of emergence. Such an ontology makes it possible to model *intrinsic constraints* on the nature and emergence of psychological processes. It makes it possible to determine not only what did develop from what was already available, but what could have developed and what could not have developed. It makes it possible to distinguish which of the relationships that have been observed are *lawful* (that is, causally necessary) and which are accidental.

The standpoint from which we seek to establish what developmental stages are, and what explanatory purposes they might serve, is a form of *realism*. Realism holds that the progress of science yields new knowledge [*Nickles*, 1980a] and leads to the discovery of new kinds of things [*Harré*, 1970]. We seek theoretical accounts of real psychological processes by which human beings interact with and represent the world, real developmental processes by which those processes can be constructed or changed, and real constraints on how those developmental processes operate. Developing adequate theories in psychology requires attention to metaphysical issues, in constructing explanations and evaluating competing theories. Appropriate explanations must make reference to levels of emergence, to underlying generative mechanisms, to essential or fundamental properties. The conceptual resources available for constructing psychological theories must be adequate to these metaphysical tasks; i.e., powerful enough to model psychological processes (see our discussion of formal modeling languages below).

Our version of realism is to be distinguished from the *instrumentalism* that pervades psychology, for the most part tacitly rather than explicitly. It is routine in science to make instrumental use of some theories whose ontological basis is questionable or flawed or has been rejected [e.g., *Shapere*, 1977]; it is not routine to regard such theories as the best possible. Instrumentalism avoids ontological claims and regards explanatory concepts as useful fictions whose sole value lies in accounting for data [for critiques of instrumentalism, see *Harré*, 1970; *Shapere*, 1977; *Wallace*, 1974].

Theoretical concepts, from the instrumentalist standpoint, make no claims about unobservable levels of reality and are not worth examining in their own right. The 'no deposit, no return' character of many of the models psychologists propose, and the lack of serious attention to the presuppositions and consequences of these models, are symptoms of instrumentalism.

Realism versus Positivism and Structuralism

Our realist approach to developmental stages aims at adequate explanations in psychology, and at methods adequate to those aims. In this regard, our approach to stages can be contrasted with the two prevailing approaches to stages: *positivism* and *structuralism*. Positivism rejects as 'metaphysical' (and therefore meaningless) any attempt to model intrinsic constraints on the emergence of unobservable processes. It permits only the use of a superficial, phenomenalistic ontology; it restricts explanation to the logical subsumption of descriptions of observable phenomena into a deductive system. To positivists [e.g., *Brainerd*, 1978], developmental stages are inadmissible unless they can be squeezed into the standard framework by regarding them as neurological antecedent conditions for behavior [*Bickhard* et al., 1985]. From our standpoint, positivism lacks true explanatory aims, and uses only weak descriptive methods of modeling.

Structuralism is, of course, the approach within which stages were originally, and usually still are, characterized. Structuralism uses more powerful descriptive methods than positivism (e.g., algebraic structures or generative grammars). It makes reference to unobservables, not just to observable behavior. It does not, however, pursue the regress toward more fundamental explanations, nor does it evaluate explanations by considerations about the nature of the system to be explained.

Structuralists tend to conflate a mathematical description of possible actions or task accomplishments with an explanation of how particular actions occur [a classic case is *Inhelder and Piaget's*, 1958, conception of the 'causality of the possible', to be discussed in Chapter 4]. A few structuralists regard their models as purely descriptive; *Commons and Richards* [1984a] consider a stage model to be a description of a hierarchy of tasks that could be solved, not an account of real psychological processes. Typically, however, structuralists do have genuine explanatory aims. *Chomsky* [1965] wanted to characterize the essential, universal properties of human languages. *Piaget* attempted to characterize mental processes, their relations to the world, and their development. Piagetian structuralism endowed the structures with internal dynamics and self-regulation: 'The structures discerned ... are viewed as self-regulating, closed, and whole, reflections of the organized human mind' [*Gardner*, 1973, p. 171]. *Piaget* [1970a, p. 14] considered his structures to be sufficient for ultimate psychological explanation, without any need to model emergence from deeper ontological levels: 'Once an area of knowledge has been reduced to a self-regulating system or "structure", the feeling that one has at last come upon its innermost source of movement is hardly avoidable.' As we will argue below, however, the formalisms employed by structuralists are only capable of describing possible task accomplishments; they are inappropriate for characterizing psychological processes and their development. Structuralism has explanatory aims, but only descriptive methods.

Models of the Organization of Lawful Process

We consider explanatory theories in general to be models of the organization of lawful process. In psychology, explanatory theories are models of the organization of synchronic psychological processes and of diachronic metaprocesses that operate on the synchronic processes. A crucial consideration is that the process language to be used in modeling psychological processes needs to be sufficiently powerful (see below); in Chapter 3 we introduce the interactive framework for modeling psychological processes, which is stated in a Turing-machine powerful language.

Lawfulness involves more than a description of patterns of regularity; for a generalization to be lawful rather than accidental, there must be a deeper ontological basis for that regularity. Lawfulness thus involves consideration of natural necessity, considerations about what kinds of things *must* happen and why. It makes reference to potentialities and to counterfactual possibilities (what would happen under other possible circumstances). (For this reason, we will argue in Chapter 4 that reasoning about laws cannot be adequately described by standard modern systems of formal logic.) It calls for explanations in terms of generative mechanisms by which a cause produces an effect, in terms of the powers of particulars which are manifested under appropriate enabling conditions. Generative mechanisms and specific powers of particulars need to be explained in terms of more fundamental properties; such explanations typically invoke multiple ontological levels of emergence and reduction. In psychology, we will argue, the concepts of developmental sequence and developmental stage pertain to *intrinsic con-*

straints [*Bickhard*, 1978] on development, to necessary constraints on emergence that derive from the nature of the developing organism.

To dispel misunderstanding, we must point out that our conception of emergence and reduction acknowledges the existence of genuinely new and different properties at the emergent level of analysis. Moreover, explaining properties at the emergent level by reduction to a more basic level of analysis does not make the emergent level dispensable or unreal. Our conception is thus to be distinguished from the eliminative reduction and epiphenomenal emergence characteristic of positivism. The conception of psychological processes as 'nothing but' brain processes is a well-known attempt at eliminative reduction. We regard (functional) psychological processes as a level of analysis distinct from (material) brain processes.

Synchronic and Diachronic Processes

In a model of psychological processes, two kinds of processes need to be distinguished. *Synchronic* processes operate at a specific point in development. The processes by which someone solves a calculus problem, or flies into a rage, or decides to order a hamburger, are synchronic processes. *Diachronic* processes operate over some span of development, and differentiate, integrate, or modify synchronic processes. Diachronic processes are also metaprocesses (because they are processes that change other processes). They are developmental processes (we use this term synonymously with the more usual 'developmental mechanisms'). The two main kinds of developmental process, we will argue, are learning (see Chapter 3) and reflective abstraction (Chapter 5). When we speak of 'process accounts' in psychology, we mean accounts of synchronic processes, and of the developmental metaprocesses that produce or alter them. (Complicating the task of psychological theory is the fact that synchronic and diachronic processes yield different orders of psychological potentiality, which must be kept distinct. Current synchronic processes for interacting with the world yield potential interactions or task accomplishments. Diachronic processes yield new, potentially constructible synchronic processes. What can be done by the knower now, and what could be learned or reflectively abstracted by the same knower, are fundamentally different. Additional contrasts between synchronic and diachronic perspectives on development are discussed in Chapter 3.)

Because developmental metaprocesses constrain what kinds of synchronic processes can develop when, they directly affect which accounts of synchronic cognitive processes are plausible. Developmental processes are integral to 'process accounts' in psychology generally. Moreover, it is important to recognize that *what actually changes or emerges in development is synchronic psychological processes.* Changes in task accomplishments, or in what can be known, are indirect manifestations of changes in synchronic processes. Learning and reflective abstraction operate on internal processes, not on the task accomplishments those processes might yield.

Descriptive Constraints on Process Explanations

Explanatory accounts of underlying processes and their properties are constrained by *descriptive* accounts of the manifestations and potentials of those processes. That is, accounts of the underlying processes that produce effects under appropriate conditions are constrained by accounts of the range of possible effects. In the case of psychological processes, which are unobservable, descriptive accounts typically take the form of characterizing task performances. These descriptions have theoretical force because they cover a potentially infinite set of possible task performances, and they are falsifiable. Such descriptions of capacity restrict explanatory theory because the explanatory theory must account for the described capacity; explanations that cannot yield the capacity have to be rejected as inadequate. However, descriptive capacity accounts are not explanations. They do not specify a generative mechanism, or an underlying process, that could produce the task accomplishments described, or account for their lawfulness. Frequently, capacity descriptions make no reference to processes at all. The basic principles used to generate descriptions of particular accomplishments are selected to maximize simplicity and notational elegance, and are unaffected by considerations of psychological reality (see below).

Capacity descriptions produce descriptive generalizations: various descriptive properties of the task accomplishments are regularly correlated with each other in various ways. However, the fundamentality or the causal relevance of these descriptive properties cannot be evaluated without constructing an explanatory model of process (see our treatment of protolaws below). An explanatory model may reveal that correlated properties have no causal relevance to one another, because they are all the result of some fundamental characteristic of an underlying process that did not enter into the description at all. The confusion of description with explanation, which is a central error of structuralism, prevails throughout psychology and related disciplines like linguistics (see Chapter 4). What develops, however, is not task accomplishments, which are manifestations of underlying processes in interaction with the environment, but the underlying processes themselves.

Forms of Explanatory Lawfulness

In this section, we discuss various kinds of explanations, moving from standard efficient causal accounts to explanations that involve progressively deeper metaphysical assumptions. In particular, we consider dispositional explanations, boundary conditions, and intrinsic constraints. We do not intend to offer an exhaustive taxonomy of kinds of explanation; instead, we aim to show that the deepest levels of ontological considerations (intrinsic constraints) are necessary for psychological explanation.

The familiar post-Humean or positivist conception restricts causal explanations to the case in which one event is the *efficient cause* of another. A classic example would be the Newtonian account of an elastic collision between two billiard balls. Two events are observed to occur in a regular pattern; the events are contiguous in space, and one (the cause) precedes the other (the effect) in time. Under the logical positivist approach, efficient causal explanations are formulated in antecedent-consequent terms: if event A occurs, then event B will occur. No reference is made to a necessary connection between events A and B. Generally, a necessary connection is not even thought to exist; an empirical regularity, or functional relation, involving logically independent events is considered sufficient.

In contrast to the standard post-Humean view, other approaches [e.g., those of *Ducasse, Bunge*, and *Bohm*; see *Wallace*, 1974] posit a necessary connection even in the standard efficient causal situation. This necessary connection has an ontological rather than a logical basis; it calls for deeper analysis of the events and of the causal relationship between them. For instance, on the generative mechanism approach [*Harré*, 1970; *Harré and Madden*, 1975], efficient causal explanations refer to enabling or inhibiting conditions on the operation of a generative causal mechanism. Efficient causal explanations are not enough; it is also necessary to know something about the powers of the particulars involved (for instance, in the case of elastic collisions, about the difference between elasticity and inelasticity) in order to know how the cause produced the effect. And an explanation of elasticity in terms of the atomic construction of the billiard balls, which involves emergence and reduction, goes even farther beyond the strict efficient causal paradigm.

Referring to *dispositional properties* (e.g., elasticity, solubility, brittleness) goes a step beyond strict efficient causal regularities. Dispositional explanations specify what something would do under certain circumstances, even if those circumstances never actually obtain. A sample of potassium chloride is soluble in water even if it never actually gets dissolved in water. Dispositional properties are not strictly 'observable' and force at least a relaxation of the strict positivist position [see *Bickhard* et al., 1985]. Structuralist accounts of developmental stages are dispositional. For instance, *Inhelder and Piaget* [1958] considered their model of formal operations to specify a set of 'structural possibilities': operations that the formal thinker could perform in some problem situation, although not all of the operations would be manifested on any particular problem. Interactive control structures are a type of disposition that is specifically relevant for functional and, therefore, psychological explanation (see Chapter 3). Dispositional explanations involve reference to potentiality and counterfactual possibility. However, it is possible for psychological dispositions to belong to different orders of potentiality, although this is not commonly recognized. Moreover, dispositions are themselves amenable to further explanation. In the generative mechanism approach, causal powers of particulars are to be explained in terms of more fundamental properties of the particulars. In other frameworks, dispositions at one ontological level may be explained by reduction to a lower ontological level.

Questions of emergence and reduction arise explicitly when *boundary conditions* are considered. Boundary conditions are a form of emergent regularity (situational or temporal) that is not equivalent to an efficient causal or dispositional relationship, but that can be explained in terms of more fundamental efficient causal and dispositional relationships. Birth order effects on personality (presuming they actually exist) are a type of boundary condition relevant to psychology. Clearly birth order is not an antecedent efficient cause of the personality differences to be explained; nor is it a dispositional property of any of the persons involved. However, the limitations or tendencies that result from birth order can presumably be explained in terms of parental experience and expectations, the possible interactions between each child and his or her siblings, etc. Boundary conditions, then, are a type of necessary relationship that derives from other types of necessary relationships. In order to deal with boundary conditions, an explanatory regress to more fundamental properties or relationships must be recognized.

Intrinsic constraints are also a form of emergent regularity, but unlike boundary constraints, they are constraints on emergence and reduction rather than situational or temporal constraints. Intrinsic constraints on development are necessary constraints that derive from the underlying nature of the developing system and the nature of the possible developmental processes. In the interactive approach to psychology, developmental sequences and stages are types of intrinsic constraints on development. Specifically, they constrain the processes and representations that can develop from those already in existence, given the nature of developmental metaprocesses and of the interactive environment. Much of the perplexity about sequences, and especially stages, has resulted from failing to recognize them as intrinsic constraints and trying to force them into impoverished frameworks for causal explanation. Sequences and stages cannot be construed as efficient causes of development. *Brainerd* [1978], from a positivist standpoint, rejected stages as explanatorily worthless; unless they could be given a neurological interpretation, stages obviously would not qualify as efficient causes [*Bickhard* et al., 1985]. More typically, sequences and stages are analyzed as dispositions, but merely analyzing them as dispositions is superficial. It leaves their descriptive or explanatory status unclear and their ground in cognitive processes and developmental metaprocesses unexplored.

Metaphysical Basis for Explanation

For those who regard explanation as a phenomenalistic description of empirical regularities, efficient causal explanations are the simplest kind. The other kinds of explanations in the sequence that we have presented (dispositional explanations, boundary conditions, intrinsic constraints) progressively add assumptions and complexities, some of these perhaps unacceptable to empiricists. From a realist standpoint, however, explanations in terms of intrinsic constraints are the most basic kind. The other kinds of explanations are (partial) applications in certain situations of the basic explanatory scheme – that what a thing (process, system) does or becomes depends on what it is. Our sequence of explanation types inverts the descriptive sequence: empirical regularities are the ultimate consequences of a complex, multilayered system of underlying relationships.

From a realist standpoint, lawfulness or necessity in causal explanations has a metaphysical basis: what things do (under specified circumstances) depends on what they are; causes and effects are connected by generative or productive mechanisms. What makes an empirical generalization a (putative) law of nature is the availability of an account of a generative mechanism, or of intrinsic constraints on the operation of a process, which explains why it obtains (we say putative because the account is presumed to be true, and it could turn out to be false). Without such a grounding, even a well-corroborated empirical generalization is at best a protolaw, and an explanation still needs to be sought for it [*Harré*, 1970].

A classic example would be *Kepler's* 'laws' of planetary motion. As stated by *Kepler*, these were correct descriptive generalizations about certain properties of the motions of the planets. However, *Kepler* was unable to provide an underlying mechanism for the regularities that he accurately described. In consequence, *Kepler's* 'laws' were only protolaws. *Newton* was able to explain *Kepler's* generalizations by deriving them from dynamics [see *Holton*, 1973; *Westfall*, 1977]; the availability of this explanation was what established them as genuine laws. Moreover, this explanation made it clear that (some of) the variables related in *Kepler's* 'laws' were themselves the results of underlying mechanisms, and so could not be actual causes of other variables to which they were related.

Campbell and Richie [1983] have shown how the distinction between laws and protolaws applies to claims about developmental sequences. Showing that children generally succeed on task A before they succeed on task B is not a sufficient basis for concluding that A and B form a developmental sequence. Such temporal orderings of task performance are at best protolaws. To establish a lawful developmental sequence, a theoretical account of the connection between success on A and success on B is needed. It is necessary to show that the process required for B could develop out of the process required for A, and that A is necessary for B to develop. The possibility that A and B belong to different sequences, but for other reasons B tends to follow A, has to be ruled out. Establishing a lawful developmental sequence requires an explanation of the sequence in terms of underlying processes and developmental metaprocesses. It requires an account of intrinsic constraints on the emergence of the ability to do task B.

What distinguishes laws from protolaws and from purely accidental generalizations, then, is the availability of an explanation for them. The necessity of laws is based on ontological considerations; it is not based on their logical syntax or their place in a formal deductive system [*Harré*, 1970; *Harré and Madden*, 1975].

Our approach to explanation and to natural necessity is to be contrasted with *Overton's* [*Overton*, 1984; *Overton and Reese*, 1981]. *Overton* considers a pure, completely static type of structuralism to be a necessary part of the 'organismic' world-view in psychology. The only basic alternative to this world-view is the 'mechanistic' world-view, characterized by physicalism, determinism, and behaviorism. *Overton* claims that only static formal explanations (like algebraic structures or rules) have necessity; explanations in terms of process must be efficient causal, and therefore contingent, or accidental. (*Overton* claims, without basis, to draw this distinction between static formal explanations and contingent process explanations from *Aristotle*. On the contrary, *Aristotle* was interested in finding necessary dynamic explanations for biological processes like growth and reproduction). The only way for process accounts to intrude into explications of development is through external, contingently varying environmental influences on what is learned when. Developmental processes, and the resultant intrinsic constraints on what can emerge from what, are not considered at all. From our standpoint, *Overton* has things exactly backwards. Descriptive generalizations like those of structuralism are not necessary per se; they require explanation to ground or establish their lawfulness. The roots of explanation, and of natural necessity, are to be found in analyses of the nature of underlying processes or generative mechanisms.

Rehabilitation of Metaphysics in Philosophy of Science

The denigration and deliberate avoidance of metaphysics in philosophy of science are rather recent developments. Medieval and early modern science were characterized by extensive metaphysical assumptions and controversies [*Buchdahl*, 1969; *Laudan*, 1977; *Wallace*, 1972, 1974]. With the rise of empiricism and positivism, philosophers attempted to exclude metaphysics from science and restrict scientific theorizing to the systematic description of empirical regularities. The collapse of the logical positivist conception of scientific theory and method [*Suppe*, 1977; *Bickhard* et al., 1985] has led to reexaminations of the history and philosophy of science from many different viewpoints. Postpositivistic philosophy of science has rehabilitated metaphysical assumptions and arguments in the generation and evaluation of scientific theories. The rejection of Humean conceptions of causality in favor of an ontologically grounded natural necessity is only part of this trend. Other philosophers have focused on the need for multiple levels of emergence and reduction [e.g., *Bohm*, 1957], and have examined how scientific domains come to be viewed as related [*Shapere*, 1977]. *Laudan* [1977] has drawn his emphasis on conceptual arguments, and on the need for theories to solve conceptual as well as empirical problems, from a historical examination of actual scientific reasoning and debate.

This trend toward the revival of metaphysics in philosophy of science has so far had little influence in psychology. Psychologists, when not in the grip of logical positivism and its corrupt variants (see our discussion of neofunctionalism below), have paid attention only to the first generation of postpositivistic philosophy of science, most notably *Kuhn* [1962] and *Lakatos* [1978]. Such philosophers recognized the importance of metaphysical assumptions in the history of science, but were reluctant to accord rationality to nonempirical arguments. Metaphysics was relegated to world-views or 'paradigms' or 'hard cores' accepted on faith. Among developmentalists, the Overton-Reese framework [e.g., *Overton*, 1984] is frequently invoked in discussions of philosophy of science [e.g., *Kail and Bisanz*, 1982]. The Overton-Reese framework is a Kuhnian conception (with some Lakatosian touches) that divides all psychological theorizing into two supposedly comprehensive, jointly exhaustive world-views: the 'mechanistic' and the 'organismic'. Not only does this classification ignore fundamental differences between types of theories (*Piaget* and *Chomsky*, constructivist and antidevelopmentalist, are both 'organismic'), the world-views are regarded as incommensurable. Rational arguments concerning their merits are impossible. This antimetaphysical position requires adherents of the Overton-Reese framework to ignore or dismiss arguments in principle concerning the power of modeling languages or the ontological commitments of theories (see below). The 'organismic' and 'mechanistic' world-views derive from a four-world-view scheme proposed by *Pepper* [1942]; the other two world-views, 'contextualism' and 'formism', sometimes appear in discussions. *Pepper's* conceptions may have some metaphorical, heuristic value in discussing theories, but they leave out vitally important issues. Adopted as rigid categories, they merely add two more false alternatives to those of the Overton-Reese model. Outside the Overton-Reese framework, straightforward appeals to Lakatosian philosophy of science are fairly common [e.g., *Pascual-Leone and Sparkman*, 1980; *Piattelli-Palmarini*, 1980; *Serlin and Lapsley*, 1985].

It is not that psychologists are altogether unfamiliar with more powerful conceptions of scientific explanation. A number of developmentalists [*Shultz*, 1982; *Bullock*, 1985; *Bullock* et al., 1982; *Koslowski*, 1983] have adopted *Harré and Madden's* [1975] generative mechanism conception as a framework for explaining the development of reasoning about physical causality. The generative mechanism approach is explicitly metaphysical; in fact, it is one of the most radical and uncompromising rejections of the

Humean conception of causality [*Wallace*, 1974]. Its proponents, unfortunately, have shied away from applying it metatheoretically to psychology. Ironically, the generative mechanism approach is considered appropriate for modeling naive thought about physics, but it is not considered relevant to sophisticated thought about psychology. *Koslowski* [1983] has used the generative mechanism conception to criticize *Piaget's* account of scientific reasoning as a formal operational procedure (see Chapter 4). If her critique applies to adolescent scientific reasoning, it ought to apply with equal merit to the conduct of psychological research itself – unless in growing up we put away metaphysics, and replace it with correlational statistics. What psychologists claim about knowledge in their developmental theories must have consequences for their views about method.

Neofunctionalism and Process Models

A standard approach to psychological research and theorizing, which *Beilin* [1983] calls neofunctionalism, acts to impede the adoption of explanatory process models. Neofunctionalism is not a fully articulated conception, and it does not correspond exactly to any one position in the philosophy of science. It is rather, as *Blanshard* [1962] said of analytic philosophy, a set of 'tendencies, tastes, and aversions', specific to psychology. Neofunctionalism draws on instrumentalism and positivism, as well as debased variants of positivism like the doctrine that all theoretical concepts must be 'operationally defined'. Textbook experimental psychology is heavily neofunctionalist, and so is most developmental research in the information-processing framework – those information-processing psychologists who are concerned about developmental processes, like *Klahr* [1984], are an exception. The neofunctionalists are suspicious of structuralist models like *Piaget's*; for them structural models are too abstract, vague, and untestable, in short, too metaphysical. By contrast, from our standpoint, structuralist models are still high-level descriptions of the data, and structuralism is not sufficiently concerned about the ontology of an explanatory theory. Our approach, then, must diverge sharply from neofunctionalism.

Neofunctionalist approaches to psychology are overwhelmingly *empiricist*: their primary focus is always on 'accounting for the data'. Any model that makes adequate empirical predictions over a narrow set of empirical problems is regarded as acceptable [*Bickhard and Richie*, 1983]. Conceptual concerns about the basis for the predictions, about the express or implied psychological ontology of the model, or about the rationale for defining and studying that class of empirical problems in the first place, are ignored. (An ironic consequence of ignoring the reasons for studying a set of problems is that anti-Piagetians frequently use Piagetian tasks, and in so doing accept all kinds of implicit presuppositions behind those tasks.) If different types of models cannot be clearly distinguished on empirical grounds, then there is no conceptual basis (such as the ontology of the models, or the power of the languages in which they are formulated) for preferring one type over another. A classic instance of this attitude is *Anderson's* [1978] response to the controversy over the type of representation ('analog' or 'propositional') that mental images might be: in the absence of clear empirical differences between models incorporating one or the other type of representation, *Anderson* concluded that the difference could not be settled, except eventually on neurological reductionist grounds.

The errors and deficiencies of neofunctionalist approaches can most often be traced to residual influences of *logical positivism* [*Kitchener*, 1983; *Bickhard* et al., 1985]. For the logical positivist, explaining a generalization consists of subsuming it logically under more general descriptive statements. The task of explanation is limited to describing contingent patterns of regularity among 'observable phenomena'. Efficient causal relations are to be described without inquiring into any deeper ontological basis for them. In fact, the ontological considerations needed for deeper explanations are to be avoided. In place of a rich, productive ontology with multiple levels of emergence, positivism seeks a 'desert landscape' ontology in which as many categories as possible are to be eliminated in favor of a restricted phenomenalistic or physicalistic base. (In psychology, radical behaviorism is the classic example of 'desert landscape' ontology.) In a 'desert landscape' ontology, necessary causal relations, along with the underlying processes and fundamental properties needed to ground them, are among the kinds of things to be rejected as 'metaphysical' or 'otiose'.

There is a strong connection between the positivist conception of explanation as *logical subsumption*, and the instrumentalist notion of theoretical concepts as 'useful fictions' [*Harré*, 1970]. If the only function of a theoretical concept in psychology is to hold a place in a formal deduction of some observational generalization, then it does not matter whether the theoretical concept pertains to anything psychologically real. Its status as a theoretical concept does not depend on ontological considerations and such considerations are, in any case, regarded as undesirable. If theoretical concepts are just useful fictions, they will not be taken seriously. Their presuppositions and consequences will not be explored. The possibility of intrinsic constraints on development will be ignored, because intrinsic constraints cannot be addressed without attempting to model psychologically real synchronic processes, and psychologically real diachronic processes that constrain their possible emergence.

The particular form of empiricist methodology characteristic of neo-functionalism might be called *dust mote inductivism*. Dust mote inductivism also derives from logical positivism and operationalism (for a brief critique of inductivism, see Chapter 3). In developmental psychology, dust mote inductivism ignores the possibility of intrinsic constraints. The focus of dust mote inductivist research is on the piecemeal examination of particular tasks, or very narrow sets of tasks. At best such research produces low-level, entirely synchronic descriptive models; considerations about underlying process and considerations about developmental mechanisms are entirely absent. Much information-processing research [e.g., *Siegler*, 1981; *Kail and Bisanz*, 1982] openly follows this pattern of building purely synchronic, task-specific models and letting developmental processes take care of themselves.

In general, inductivism ignores conceptual or ontological constraints on theory-construction and evaluation. Meaningful patterns of regularity are thought to emerge directly from collections of empirical data. Establishing a causal relation is thought to be a matter of finding variables that are consistently correlated, and ruling out 'spurious' relations by appropriate experimental or analytic techniques. This conception of causality, which prevails in discussions of methodology, presupposes the reduction of causal relations to mathematical functional relations. Equating causal and functional relations was a cornerstone of positivism, traceable to *Mach*. It was also one of the first claims to be rejected by postpositivistic philosophy of science [*Wallace*, 1974]. Developmentalists who construe causality in terms of generative mechanisms, especially *Shultz* [1982], have argued that causal relations and functional relations are distinct even for young children. The professional methodologists have so far remained impervious to these trends.

Dust mote inductivism seriously distorts conceptions that pertain to intrinsic constraints on development, such as developmental sequences and stages. Establishing a developmental sequence is thought to be a matter of finding consistent empirical orderings of performance on tasks of increasing structural complexity: a 'psychometric' model of sequence determination [*Siegler*, 1981; *Fischer*, 1980]. Such procedures are inherently inadequate. The best they can yield (when they do not yield accidental generalizations) is protolaws, because the underlying synchronic and diachronic processes that produce the described patterns are not modeled or considered [*Campbell and Richie*, 1983]. Inductivism distorts developmental stages in comparable ways, as we will show in Chapter 4. Stages cannot be construed as intrinsic constraints on the outcomes of developmental processes, so they are reduced to descriptive regularities of task performance (temporal homogeneity or task-descriptive homogeneity).

Neofunctionalist attitudes in general have seriously impaired the credibility of psychology in related disciplines like logic, epistemology, and linguistics. Philosophers and linguists have presumed that 'empirical psychology' cannot produce any understanding of necessity, and so cannot meaningfully constrain philosophical and linguistic theorizing. In consequence, philosophy and linguistics have generally been viewed as autonomous disciplines that do not depend on psychology, even though language, knowledge, and reasoning are obviously part of the subject matter of psychology. Theories in psychology, as in any other discipline, make ontological claims, and by virtue of their ontological claims, do indicate what is necessary and constrain what is possible. It is because most psychologists have not taken ontology seriously that they have failed to have any impact on linguistics and philosophy.

Metatheoretical Intrinsic Constraints: The Power of Modeling Languages

Intrinsic Constraints and Modeling Language Constraints

The exploration of intrinsic constraints on a phenomenon, already unusual in psychology, introduces another level of considerations that are virtually ignored: considerations about metaconstraints on the language being used to model that phenomenon. In this section, we will discuss considerations about metaconstraints, and develop some of their implications for psychological modeling. We will outline the connection between intrinsic constraints and modeling language constraints, and then discuss two modeling language constraints that are especially relevant.

The first step from intrinsic constraints toward model language constraints has already been discussed. Exploring intrinsic constraints requires reasoning about the ontology of the phenomenon in question, because the intrinsic constraints are precisely constraints intrinsic to that ontology. Such reasoning about ontology, in turn, requires a model of that ontology; and such a model must be constructed within some modeling language. Reason-

ing about intrinsic constraints, thus, must occur in the language that is being
used to model the ontology that might manifest those intrinsic constraints.
At this point the possibility of constraints on the modeling language becomes
directly relevant. Any constraints on the modeling power of the language will
be imposed on the models that use that language. The danger arises that these
constraints will be considered inherent to the ontology of the phenomenon
being modeled.

Two possible problems emerge from this connection between constraints on the language and constraints on the specific models that get constructed within it. First, the constraints on the modeling language might not
be understood or might be ignored. In consequence, a specific model (in fact,
any model in that language) could be intrinsically incapable of modeling the
phenomenon, unbeknownst to the investigator. Second, the constraints on
the modeling language might be discovered, but misinterpreted. They could
be interpreted as intrinsic constraints on the ontology of the phenomenon
being modeled, instead of modeling constraints on the language being used.
Modeling language constraints may be confused with modeled intrinsic constraints.

So far, we have focused on the connection between particular models
and the modeling language within which they are constructed. The issues
raised, however, hold even more strongly for *types* of models when those
types are defined, either implicitly or explicitly, by the modeling language
within which they are constructed. Research programs are often organized
around types of models defined by their modeling languages. The confusion
between properties of the language and properties of the phenomenon can
distort entire research programs, or even make them useless. The effects of
modeling language constraints are even more likely to be missed or misinterpreted when a research program rather than a single model is being evaluated. Inadequacies or questionable properties in a single model, or the finite
set of models that have already been explored, can be attributed to particular
drawbacks of those models that will disappear when the program has
developed further. For instance, advocates of the information-processing
approach to cognitive development may acknowledge that current information-processing models are narrowly task-specific and fail to specify how
development occurs. Proponents of the approach argue that these defects are
not inherent in the framework and will disappear when more sophisticated
models are constructed [*Kail and Bisanz*, 1982]. We will argue (see Chapter
3) that these deficiencies are indeed inherent in the information-processing
framework (most basically, because it treats mental processes as computa-

tions operating on encoded representations). We will also illustrate other examples of frameworks in psychology whose inherent limitations have generally gone unrecognized.

Certain philosophies of science that have become popular with developmental psychologists appear to present a direct obstacle to metatheoretical considerations about modeling languages. In particular, world-view philosophies of science, such as those of *Kuhn* [1962] and *Lakatos* [1978], ignore or actively rule out any evaluation of theoretical frameworks along the lines we are discussing. For instance, in *Lakatos'* approach, sets of related theories, or 'research programs', share a common 'hard core' of assumptions that are held immune from refutation of any kind. Research programs develop through progressive modification of a 'protective belt' of auxiliary hypotheses surrounding the hard core; new specific models are generated to deal with empirical anomalies that refute prior models. The only basis for rationally rejecting a research program is if it is manifestly 'degenerating'; that is, interesting specific models are no longer being produced. *Lakatos'* approach grudgingly acknowledges the necessity of metaphysical assumptions for scientific theorizing, but denies that such assumptions can be rationally criticized. Only empirical refutations are acceptable. As a purported historical account, the Lakatosian view is clearly false; disputes about metaphysical questions, not just about data, pervade the history of science [*Buchdahl*, 1969; *Wallace*, 1972, 1974; *Laudan*, 1977]. *Lakatos* has been severely criticized for ignoring the role of conceptual problems and arguments in theory evaluation [*Suppe*, 1977; *Laudan*, 1977]. To the extent that developmental psychologists accept world-view philosophies of science [e.g., *Piattelli-Palmarini*, 1980; *Pascual-Leone and Sparkman*, 1980; *Overton*, 1984; *Serlin and Lapsley*, 1985], they will be condemned to keep constructing new models within modeling frameworks whose conceptual deficiencies they do not allow themselves to evaluate.

Modeling Languages for Psychological Processes

The most basic ontology appropriate for psychological explanation is the ontology of process. Psychological phenomena are emergent phenomena of special kinds of processes [*Bickhard*, 1980a, b; *Bickhard and Richie*, 1983]. Psychological understanding must ultimately rest on some form of process explication. In psychology, issues about properties of modeling languages pertain most fundamentally to languages of process as they might be used in psychological theorizing. The details of an appropriate ontology of psychological processes are highly complex; some of them will be addressed in

Chapter 3. In order to model such processes, whatever their details, a general language of process will be required.

There are many languages of process, and new ones being developed continuously. The general field of process languages is referred to variously as the theory of computation, the theory of abstract machines, recursive function theory, programming theory, and so on. Each of these terms emphasizes one perspective on process over others, and within each perspective are many languages and mathematical results. There is no dearth of choices when seeking a language for process models.

There is a natural distinction within this realm of process languages, however, that is directly relevant to the modeling power issues that we wish to discuss. The distinction is based on Turing's thesis (equivalently: Church's thesis). Turing's thesis posits that any effectively specifiable formal procedure can be realized by a Turing machine [*Rogers*, 1967]. For our purposes, this is equivalent to the thesis that the language of Turing machine theory is capable of modeling any possible process whatsoever [there is an important caveat in *Bickhard and Richie*, 1983, note 23]. The distinction that this introduces is based on the fact that there are many process languages equivalent in modeling power to Turing machine theory: any process modelable in Turing machine theory is modelable in these other languages, and vice versa. There are also many process languages that are of lesser modeling power. The distinction, then, is between languages that are Turing-machine powerful and those that are not. This distinction is crucial because there are no known effective limits on the power of Turing-machine powerful languages to model formal processes, while there are precisely specifiable limits for languages that are not Turing-machine powerful. Turing-machine powerful and non-Turing-machine powerful languages pose different types of problems.

Non-Turing-Machine Powerful Languages

Most fundamentally, any language that is not Turing-machine powerful suffers from intrinsic limits on the possible power of any model constructed within it. If a particular phenomenon exceeds the power of such a language, then no model within that language can adequately account for the phenomenon. Conversely, any such model or model type will manifest constraints that are *not* properties of the phenomenon.

Furthermore, such modeling constraints *cannot* be discovered within the program of constructing improved models using the same intrinsically limited language. Any failures of such models will be attributed to the models per se, and taken as errors to correct in the next phase of model building. That is, such constraints on the modeling power of the language cannot be discovered empirically – only a metatheoretical analysis of the language itself will reveal them. For process languages, only a mathematical comparison with Turing-machine powerful languages will specify the degree and form of limitation involved.

A classic example of this point is *Chomsky's* [1959] argument that associationistic psychology lacks the power to model language processes. Associationistic psychology is fundamentally committed to models that can be constructed in a language of S's and R's and hyphens. The commitment to such a language derives from the commitment to the corresponding exclusive ontology of stimuli, responses, and associations among them. A devastating critique of the adequacy of this whole program involves a metamodeling result: no possible model in such a modeling language can account for obvious properties of language learning. Even with highly generous assumptions about the rate of learning, there are so many associations required to account for the known dependencies involved that it would take vast ages to learn them. Constructing and testing particular associationistic models would never reveal this limitation in principle – it can only be discovered by a metatheoretical analysis. (As we noted above, this kind of argument in principle is impermissible from a Kuhnian or Lakatosian standpoint, because it is a critique of the 'hard core' of associationism. From such a standpoint [e.g., *Overton*, 1984], all that we can do is arbitrarily choose our world-view and let the associationists choose theirs. Eventually, the associationists may lose interest in constructing new associationistic models and abandon their program. The obscurantism – and historical inaccuracy – of the world-view approach should be obvious.)

A standard fallback defense of associationistic models is a version of Ockham's razor: do not invoke a more complex type of model for any particular phenomenon unless it is known that a simpler type of model, i.e., an associationistic model, cannot suffice. For psychological theory in general, however, this is a direct violation of Ockham's razor. Once it is known that more complex forms of models are required for, say, language learning, then it is a violation of simplicity to introduce an additional form of model – associationism – for something that the more complex form of model is already capable of handling.

The only defense for such a move would be an ontological one – to claim that the ontology of S's and R's and hyphens is psychologically real for the phenomenon of interest, and must therefore be accounted for in the model. Ontological defenses of insufficiently powerful models are rarely presented.

Instead, we usually find an instrumentalist defense that such models are useful in predicting or accounting for some phenomena. Completely nontechnical models stated in ordinary English can be defended in the same manner, and the problems are the same in both cases. Purely instrumental, metaphorical models are known to be wrong, but the knowledge of the limits on their useful application is purely ad hoc and piecemeal. Instrumental models provide no basis for exploring intrinsic constraints; instrumental models provide no basis for exploring possible emergences; instrumental models provide no basis for understanding why things happen the way they do; and so on. In general, the ontological commitments of a modeling language are just as important as its general modeling power.

A second example of failure to recognize metalimitations in the modeling power of a modeling language is given by the history of Perceptrons. Perceptrons are a type of model of perceptual pattern recognition. They consist of a grid of 'retinal' cells which detect points of light and generate corresponding signals, which are then processed in a generally specified way to yield a resultant signal classifying the overall pattern on the grid as belonging to a specified type of pattern or not. Many Perceptrons were built and simulated, and it appeared that slow but incremental progress was being made. This research program continued from the late fifties up to the publication of *Minsky and Papert's* [1969] examination of Perceptrons. Perceptrons as a type of model are characterized by the form of processing of the retinal signals, that is, by the forms of mathematical language for such processing that can be used to construct them. Instead of defining still another Perceptron model, *Minsky and Papert* explored the modeling capabilities of this general form of modeling language and were able to prove that there were significant, humanly recognizable, patterns that no possible Perceptron could recognize. That is, they proved that the modeling language being used was intrinsically limited in a way that made it incapable of modeling human pattern recognition capabilities. No amount of empirical exploration of particular Perceptron models could have discovered this limitation.

In general, using non-Turing-machine powerful languages is a dangerous and confusing practice. It conflates two fundamentally different sources of modeling errors: errors in the specifics of the model, and limitations of the language of the model. Non-Turing-machine powerful modeling languages should be used only when there is explicit and good reason to believe that the modeling language is appropriate to the modeling task at hand – in particular, when there is explicit and good reason to believe that the ontological assumptions and capacities of the language are appropriate to the ontology of the phenomenon being modeled. Such metatheoretical choices of modeling languages need explicit metatheoretical justifications. The prevalence of instrumentalist conceptions of theory in psychology, however, leads to a lack of serious interest in the ontological assumptions of the approaches to modeling being used. The logical positivist empiricist bias of much of contemporary psychology [*Kitchener*, 1983; *Bickhard* et al., 1985] also leads psychologists to disregard metatheoretical questions. In so doing, they run the risk of becoming locked into research programs or theoretical frameworks that are inherently inadequate to model psychological processes.

Turing-Machine Powerful Languages

Theoretical modeling within Turing-machine powerful languages does not encounter the problem of modeling limitations imposing themselves on the exploration. If a formal process cannot be modeled within a Turing-machine powerful language, then it is not a possible formal process – and that is an ontological impossibility, not just a modeling impossibility. In other words, the modeling limitations of Turing-machine powerful languages are realizations of intrinsic limitations on the ontology of formal process.

Issues involving the more specific ontological assumptions of the modeling language, however, are just as important for Turing-machine equivalent languages as for any other. In fact, the issue of ontological assumptions, the issue of psychological reality, takes on a new level of importance when modeling with maximally powerful languages.

Most importantly, when freely constructing a model within a maximally powerful language, the ability to account for the data in a given study (or finite set of studies) with such a model is mathematically guaranteed by the power of the modeling language. Therefore, accounting for the data has no selection power whatsoever among the myriads of possible models within the many available Turing-machine powerful modeling languages that could equally well account for the same data. Accounting for the data with a freely constructed model in a maximally powerful language is simply an instance of a mathematically necessary fact. It is a necessary condition for the model to be considered, but it is not sufficient to provide any confirmatory weight at all to similar language defined model types – it is guaranteed that such models will exist within any maximally powerful language.

Post production rules, for example, form a maximally powerful modeling language that has become favored by some in language studies and developmental modeling. Production rules are Turing-machine powerful, and are thus certain to be able to provide a model accounting for any particu-

3. The Interactive Model

Interactivism

Interactivism is an approach to all of psychology. In Chapter 2, we stressed the fundamental importance of psychological ontology to psychology. Correspondingly, interactivism is defined in terms of its ontology. At the root, interactivism is a commitment to a psychological ontology of abstract process and process emergents [*Bickhard*, 1982; *Bickhard and Richie*, 1983]. As such, it has radical repercussions throughout psychology. Contemporary psychology, even when it appears to be strongly process-oriented, still constructs models that depend on ontologies of substance and static structure (supplemented by agents conceived as homunculi). Homunculus models simply presuppose the phenomena of agency, intention, planning, etc., that they are supposed to explicate. Similarly, substance and static structural models presuppose the properties of persistence, invariance, and rigidity in organizations of psychological processes that are most in need of explication. Still worse, structural ontologies commonly distort functional and process properties into structural properties, thereby falsely imputing such substance-structural characteristics as componential atomism [e.g., *Wittgenstein's*, 1961, logical atomist model of linguistic meaning], efficient causal types of interrelation [e.g., *Fodor and Pylyshyn's*, 1981, model of perceptual transduction], and so on, to functional and process phenomena for which such properties are totally inappropriate.

Dependence on structural ontologies is deeply manifested, for example, in the standard conceptions of mental representation. It is almost universally assumed that representation is fundamentally some sort of 'thing' (entity, structure, event, even process) that *encodes*, or stands in a structural correspondence relation with, some other 'thing', and which represents that second 'thing' precisely by virtue of the structural correspondence with it. Encoding assumptions about representation permeate all of psychology. The interactive ontology requires that representation be explicated at a deeper level than encodings, and, thus, in this one instance alone, requires radical changes in virtually every subdomain of psychology.

Interactive approaches have been extended to a number of subdomains of psychology, at varying levels of detail. The nature of representation has been deeply explored [*Bickhard*, 1980b; *Bickhard and Richie*, 1983]. The foundational psychological processes of knowing, learning, emotions, and consciousness, and their evolutionary emergence have been given a preliminary explication [*Bickhard*, 1980a]. Higher level individual developments such as language and the emergence of social reality have been explicated [*Bickhard*, 1980b, in press; *Bickhard and Campbell*, in press]. Central higher level considerations such as personality and psychopathology have begun to be analyzed [*Bickhard*, 1985, in preparation].

The theoretical developments most pertinent to this monograph rest on the interactive ontology of representation and knowing. The standard encoding ontology for representation is fundamentally flawed, and the interactive alternative leads very naturally to a conception of developmental stages and developmental process that is not available within the encoding perspective. In fact, stronger claims can be made: the encoding conception is *logically incoherent* when examined at its roots, and the interactive alternative *logically forces* a model of developmental stages that cannot even be stated within the encoding framework.

The topics given most attention in this introduction to the interactive model will thus be representation and knowing. They are the foundation of the developmental model to be elaborated in the rest of the monograph. The nature of consciousness also plays a critical, though subordinate role. Those parts of the model beyond the developmental aspect cannot be elaborated in this monograph, and those peripheral to the core issues of representation and knowing will be particularly condensed.

The Nature of Representation

Representation is standardly considered to be some form of encoding. Encoding elements are representations insofar as some epistemic agent knows what they represent. An encoding element *is* an encoding element in virtue of an epistemic connection between that element and something else, which it thus represents via that epistemic connection. There is no problem with this encoding form of representation for paradigmatic cases, such as ciphers and computer codes. Ciphers and computer codes are encodings

tion that in fact succeeds in interacting with the environment, and in differentiating it in usable ways. The only possible source of such new system organization is internal to the system (as long as we are not considering externally designed and built systems). Learning, therefore, must be modeled as an internal process of system construction. Similarly, there is no way for such a constructive process to anticipate with certainty *which* new system organizations will be useful. It could not do so unless it already had the knowledge in question. Learning, therefore, must involve the ability to make errors, and, correspondingly, to correct them. Learning involves a constructive process of trying out new system organization, and selecting out those new trials that do not produce successful interaction and differentiation. Learning must at root involve a metaprocess of constructive variation and selection, a process that varies and selects interactive process organizations. Interactivism, then, *necessitates* constructivism, in the sense that the ontology of learning is intrinsically constrained to be constructivist in nature (constructivism, however, does not necessitate interactivism: foundational encodings could, presumably, also be constructed if they were not impossible on other grounds). *Popper* [1965] and *Campbell* [1974] have emphasized the elimination of errors and the quasi-evolutionary aspects of learning; *von Glasersfeld* [1981, 1984] has pointed out the quasi-evolutionary and constructivist aspects of learning, and emphasized their deep relationship to Piagetian constructivism.

In the interactive view, the constructive process operates on the organization of the system, while representation is an aspect of that system. In particular, the 'elements' of construction are elements of process organization – there are no elements of representation. Representation and knowledge are constructed indirectly via new system organization rather than directly in terms of basic elements of representation (encodings). There is no bound on the potentialities of system organization, and thus no combinatoric bound on the potentialities of knowledge and representational power [by contrast, the encoding conception places sharp bounds on human representational power; see *Fodor*, 1981, 1983]. There is no logical problem with constructing fundamentally new knowledge within the interactive perspective.

Similarly, there is no logical problem with differentiating learning and development within the interactive perspective. Learning is the (specific) *synchronic* aspect of the process of constructing new system organization, and development is the (universal) *diachronic* aspect of that process. Learning is the synchronic aspect of the constructive metaprocess. Typical issues about learning are what stimulates attempts at new construction, what influences the nature of the variations that are attempted, and what the process of selection is. Development is the diachronic aspect of the constructive metaprocess – its tendencies over time, and the intrinsic constraints on it (for a discussion of intrinsic constraints, see Chapter 2). Developmental issues include the system organizations and constructive trajectories of system organizations that can be expected over time, the intrinsic, environmental, and innate explanations available for such organizations and trajectories, and the sequential organization of such trajectories and the nature of domains in which they occur [e.g., *Campbell and Richie*, 1983; *Richie*, 1984].

Such developmental questions have no interesting answers in the encoding approach because it lacks intrinsic constraints that would provide any regularities in such long-term constructive properties. Encodingism provides only a synchronic constraint on possible combinations of basic encodings. The synchronic combinatorial constraint yields only one intrinsic diachronic tendency: the construction of new encodings over time should move from particular to general, from elemental encodings to progressively more composite encodings. This epistemological inductivism was an assumption of logical positivism (long since abandoned), and still influences psychology. Inductivism is grounded in an incoherent conception of basic encodings (see above), and it is empirically false. Development differentiates as much as it abstracts; it moves from the general to the particular as much as it moves from the particular to the general. The only additional constraints available from the encoding approach are the initial set of innate basic encodings, and the environments to which the individual is exposed. Both are enabling or inhibiting conditions contingent to the developmental process, not aspects intrinsic to it; both are constraints on what might ultimately be learned, not on the developmental process or trajectory per se. Developmental questions, then, get sparse and false answers from encodingism. Development in its full sense – the construction of fundamentally new knowledge and powers of thought – is simply not possible according to the encoding perspective.

Within the interactive approach, it does no harm to refer loosely to the constructive process per se as the learning process. Being careful, however, to maintain the formal distinction between learning and development as different *aspects* of a single underlying process has explanatory advantages. It explicates directly how learning and development are intimately related, yet not the same, and how the questions in each area seem to merge into one another. It also explains why learning tends to focus more on individual differences and development more on universals. Specific instances of metaconstruction are situationally dependent, and new content is largely determined by the particulars of the environment; interesting generalizations are available primarily in terms of individual differences in response to varied environments. By contrast, constructive tendencies over time tend to be relatively independent of particular environments, and thus more universal to the constructive process itself. Neither of these alternatives is absolute, but the reason for the discerned tendencies nevertheless seems clear.

Developmental Stages and Processes

The interactive ontology provides a major intrinsic constraint on the course of development that is the central topic of this monograph: an intrinsically necessary structure of stages of development. To this point, we have discussed knowing and representation only with respect to an external environment. But the knowing system itself has properties that might be useful to know, and interesting constraints emerge when the possibility of knowing these properties is examined. Specifically, the level of the system that interactively knows the environment cannot directly know itself – knowing is intrinsically irreflexive. That first system level *can*, however, be known by a second level interacting with the first. Such a second level of the system, in turn, will have properties that could be known from a third level, and so on. Thus, the interactive perspective intrinsically generates a sequence of possible levels of knowing. That sequence intrinsically constrains development to a corresponding sequence of stages. No metaconstructive process could generate a level of knowing out of sequence, because a level of knowing with no system level of knowing immediately below it would have nothing to know, and, therefore, could not exist. Development, therefore, must proceed up the levels of knowing in strict sequence [*Bickhard*, 1978, 1980a]. The developmental consequences of the levels of knowing, and of the stage sequence which they generate, form the core of the developmental analyses in this monograph.

There are two parts to the derivation of this hierarchy of levels of knowing: the irreflexivity of knowing, and the assumption that there are properties to be known at a given level of knowing. Irreflexivity follows from the interactive explication of knowing in terms of an interactive system differentiating and implicitly defining categories outside of itself – the interactive, differentiating, and implicit definitional relationships are all intrinsically irreflexive. The assumption that there is new knowledge to be known at new levels of knowing follows from the fact that representation and knowing are *aspects* of interactive systems: there will always be implicit properties of knowing systems and their organization that are not explicitly known by those knowing systems, but could be known by examining those systems from a higher level.

Encodings, in contrast, have no implicit functional properties. They are constituted by their having a representational content, and that is their entire functional essence. (Encodings may have further material properties, but these would have at best accidental relationships to the encodings' representational contents and organizations.) There is nothing to be known from any higher level except perhaps the representational content of the encodings, but that was already *explicit* in those encodings in the first place. If a higher level of encodings were to emerge (and it might, e.g., for reasons of efficiency), the encodings at this higher level would have to encode the same things as those at the lower level (though perhaps in a different form). The encoding relationship is transitive: 'X' encodes Y, and 'Y' encodes Z, implies that 'X' encodes Z. Therefore, levels of encodings collapse epistemically. No level can escape the combinatorial constraint that already applies at the first level. Nothing like the knowing levels and corresponding stages can be defined within the encoding perspective.

Interactivism also provides an ontology for a specifically developmental process – reflective abstraction. Reflective abstraction is the process by which properties inherent in one level of knowing come to be known at the next level. This process will not be explicated here (see Chapter 5), but two points can be made. First, as we showed above, the transitivity of encodings, their lack of implicit functional properties, and the strict combinatorial constraints on them rule out reflective abstraction. Reflective abstraction is impossible within the encoding view – it cannot even be defined. Second, reflective abstraction will turn out to be a specialized emergent from the general metaconstructive process already discussed. As such, it will have synchronic, i.e., learning, aspects. It also illustrates the general possibility for implicit properties of an interactive system to become explicit in specialized, dedicated subsystems [see the discussions of the origins and development of language in *Bickhard*, 1980b, and of derivative encodings and associated systems in *Bickhard and Richie*, 1983, for further examples].

A Macroevolutionary Sequence:
Knowing, Learning, Emotions, Consciousness

We have explicated knowing in terms of the interactions of certain systems, including living systems. We have explicated learning in terms of constructive metaprocesses on underlying knowing (living) systems. Any living

in terms of the detection properties of those interactions, then we tend to call those interactions 'perceptual'.

This interactive conception contrasts strongly with the standard encoding view of perception. In the standard view, sensations are encoded; sensations are then augmented with extra information to generate encoded perceptions. Perception is considered a separate process that 'feeds' information to, and uses information from, cognition. The encoding view of perception runs up against the incoherence of foundational encodings in several ways. It requires that the sensations be transduced as encodings. Transduction is impossible; it presupposes knowledge of which sensation-encoding to transductively generate, and of what it encodes once generated, and these requirements iterate to form an infinite regress. The presumed encoding transduction cannot in fact epistemically reach across the boundary of the perceptual system to see what it is encoding. The standard view of perception also requires cognitive information about what information to add to sensations. This cognitive information is presumed to be derived from prior perceptions, which are derived from still prior cognitions, deriving from even more prior perceptions, etc. – the origin of the cognitive information that enhances perceptions is lost in an infinite regress. Moreover, the standard view requires that the information in the resultant perceptual encodings be interpreted (i.e., known). Yet the model of perception was supposed to explain how that information about the environment was known in the first place. Perception of the environment gets lost in an infinite regress of homunculi interpreting, perceiving, the indirectly generated perceptions [*Bickhard and Richie*, 1983]. In the interactive view, perception may be a physically differentiated process (as in the visual and auditory systems), but it is functionally and logically an aspect of the basic knowing process.

In a discussion of developmental stages, it is worth remarking how the standard view of perception distorted *Piaget's* account of development. *Piaget's* conception of 'operative' knowing incorporated genuine interactive insights (although his formal structural models intended to explain operative knowing did not – see Chapter 4). *Piaget* never attempted, however, to analyze perception in operative terms. Instead, he accepted the standard static, sensation-based encoding account of perception, and treated it as a distinct 'figurative' type of knowledge. At the same time, however, *Piaget* was aware of some of the inadequacies of static encodings as a type of knowledge. In consequence, he rejected perception as an inferior type of knowledge, divorced perception from active interactions with the world, and denied that it could be a source of 'operative' development. The interactive model restores the essential connection between perception and action, and puts perception back on the main pathways of development.

Language

The nonencoding ontology for representation that interactivism provides has important consequences for all areas of cognitive psychology. Memory, for instance, is conventionally thought to be the organization, association, and storage of encodings. Problem-solving is standardly conceived as manipulations and computations on encoded spaces of representations. Nowhere, however, does the interactive model have a deeper impact than on standard models of language.

In standard approaches, language is the encoding of mental contents (themselves encodings) into a signal to be transmitted to a recipient, who then decodes that signal into corresponding mental contents. The study of language is customarily divided into syntax (the rules for well-formed encodings), semantics (the rules for the encoding relationships), and pragmatics (the ways in which such encoded utterances can be used). The incoherence of foundational encodings infects this view of language throughout. No part of it is possible or even makes sense from the interactive perspective.

The interactive model of language cannot be developed here. Briefly, utterances are understood to be interactive operations on social realities that emerge from the representational processes and organizations of the individuals involved as utterer or audience [*Bickhard*, 1980b, in press; *Bickhard and Campbell*, in press]. Among the consequences of this model: semantics and pragmatics cannot be coherently defined in the standard manner; syntax cannot have the kind of autonomy it is often assumed and argued to have; language is intrinsically context-dependent in all circumstances, not just occasionally and removably so as in standard views; propositional analyses of language, and truth conditional approaches to meaning, cannot be carried out; and so on. There are also deep implications for language development [*Bickhard*, 1980b, in press].

Other Higher Order Processes

In Chapter 8, we will present brief explications of the self, identity, and values. Little can be said here about other higher order psychological processes like attitudes, moods, personality, and psychopathology. The interactive commitment to a process ontology, however, affects these areas as well. It will not do to treat attitudes as having encoded objects. Structural conceptions of personality and its organization are inappropriate: for instance, the division into id, ego, and superego, or into a structural conscious and an unconscious populated with independent homunculi. Nor can personality be characterized by introjected object encodings, or encoded irrational beliefs, or associations between encoded stimuli and responses. Structural taxonomies of psychopathological dysfunctions are also deficient. The interactive perspective on these areas will be developed elsewhere [*Bickhard*, 1985, in preparation].

Our emphasis in this chapter has been on how the interactive approach deals with cognitive representation and developmental metaprocesses. We have thus laid the groundwork for an account of developmental stages in terms of knowing levels. In Chapter 4, we will develop the knowing-level conception of stages and contrast it with Piagetian and neo-Piagetian structural stage models. Specifically, we will contrast knowing level 3 with *Piaget's* stage of formal operations. We will criticize defenses of structural stage models in terms of the Chomskyan competence-performance distinction. We will analyze standard properties of structural stages, like temporal homogeneity, and show that knowing-level stages need not have these properties. In general, we will argue that structural stages are attempts to describe classes of possible task performances. Structural stages have no explanatory value. Piagetian and post-Piagetian structures cannot model cognitive processes (they are static) and cannot adequately model representation (they are structures of encodings). The developmental process of reflective abstraction cannot be defined in terms of foundational encodings and has no place in a structural stage model. Knowing-level stages, grounded in an interactive approach to cognition, avoid these difficulties.

4. A Critique of Structural Stage Models

Whether there are stages in psychological development has been the subject of protracted controversy. By stages, we mean invariantly sequenced, qualitatively distinct levels that can meaningfully characterize developmental sequences of abilities across domains. Stages pertain to intrinsic, sequential constraints on development: they constrain what further abilities can be readily constructed, given the nature of developmental metaprocesses, and the present abilities of the knower. *Piaget*, of course, maintained that there were stages, and that they could be characterized by means of algebraic *structures*. Concrete operational thought was formally characterized in terms of the nine groupings; formal operational thought was characterized in terms of the combinatorial and the INRC group. *Piaget's* structural stages have come under severe criticism, especially for the claim that all of the structures characteristic of a stage must be present for any of them to be present (the doctrine of structures of the whole). There have been numerous attempts to replace *Piaget's* stages with a system that predicts empirical task accomplishments better, and that avoids overly strong claims of synchrony between task accomplishments across domains. Such neo-Piagetian and post-Piagetian models, however, continue to describe stages in terms of structures, like mappings and systems of mappings [*Fischer*, 1980] or dimensional task analyses [*Pascual-Leone*, 1980; *Case*, 1978]. Critical attacks on the viability of stages [e.g., *Flavell*, 1982] presume that stages are structurally defined.

There is, however, a different approach that does not define stages in terms of structures. As *Bickhard* [1978, 1980a] has shown, it is possible to define developmental stages in terms of a hierarchy of *levels of knowing* that is generated by iterating the basic knowing relationship. (The basis for this hierarchy in the interactive model of knowing was explicated in Chapter 3). The hierarchy of knowing levels has an invariant sequence, and can be applied to any developmental sequence in any domain. The knowing levels can thus be used as the basis for a new, nonstructural definition of stages.

An important reason for attempting a nonstructural account is that developmental psychology needs a process-relevant account of stages if abstraction is the process by which level-3 abilities are constructed. Judgments of logical sufficiency and insufficiency (ALC) are an early indication of reflection on level-2 inferences, hence of level-3 abilities. The third criterion, MIS, we do not regard as fundamental for knowing-level differences – it is mostly a problem complexity measure. By contrast, stage conceptions that are not based on knowing levels often define stages in terms of the number of dimensions that can be coordinated [*Fischer*, 1980; *Pascual-Leone*, 1980; *Case*, 1978]. Unfortunately, although *Lunzer* was a very early advocate of reflective abstraction as the mechanism of transition through the Piagetian stages [see his introduction to *Inhelder and Piaget*, 1964], he did not go on to challenge and redefine *Piaget's* stage boundaries. Because he took success on *Inhelder and Piaget's* [1958] scientific reasoning tasks as the benchmark of formal operational thought, he perforce concluded that ALC and abstraction were only prerequisites for formal operational reasoning, which needed extra ingredients like MIS.

Structural Stages as Competence Models

The Competence-Performance Distinction

At this point we must respond to a common defense of formal operations. The *competence-performance* distinction is often invoked to defend structural stage models against empirical criticism. Such models are said to be *competence* models [*Neimark*, 1979; *Stone and Day*, 1980; *Broughton*, 1981a; *Overton and Newman*, 1982]. Competence models are abstract models of general knowledge of a domain. They are not sufficient to explain the behavior of individuals in varied task situations. A model of *performance* factors that evoke, inhibit, or moderate competence is also needed to account for actual task accomplishments. Thus the heterogeneous accomplishments actually observed on Piagetian tasks are not grounds for rejecting the structural stage model. They are to be explained by supplementing it with appropriate performance models. For instance, advocates of the competence-performance distinction deny that empirical questions about the use of all 16 binary operations [*Bynum* et al., 1972; *Weitz*, et al., 1973] have any bearing on the adequacy of the combinatorial. At best, such evidence indicates that performance models must be adjusted to explain why not all 16 operations are normally manifested in problem-solving [*Broughton*, 1981a; *Tomlinson-Keasey*, 1982].

We contend that the competence-performance distinction is based on fundamental errors and that invoking it in defense of Piagetian structural stage models only perpetuates the deficiencies of such models. The competence-performance distinction conflates systematic *descriptions* of human task accomplishments with *explanations* of how those tasks are accomplished. (On the description-explanation issue, see Chapter 2 and *Bickhard and Campbell*, in preparation.) It leads to serious distortions in developmental research and theory evaluation: A permanent segregation of mental processes and representations into a 'competence' class and a 'performance' class, with the former enjoying logical priority; an attempt to make structural stage models immune to conceptual criticism as well as empirical criticism; and the exclusion of developmental processes from the 'competence' model and hence from the core of developmental theory. The study of development in general, and the stage question in particular, would benefit if the competence-performance distinction were rejected.

Underlying Abilities and Extraneous Factors

The intuitive notion of competence in psychology is that children or adults can do things that are not manifested in their performance on particular tasks, but might be manifested under different circumstances. We have no quarrel with this intuitive distinction; it is consistent with our own conception of competence as an aspect of the knowing system (Chapter 3). We do want to point out that the standard competence-performance dichotomy does not follow from it. The intuitive notion is pretheoretical and does not dictate how psychological processes should be modeled. It does not clearly distinguish possible task accomplishments from the processes by which the tasks could be accomplished, but it does not conflate them either. The intuitive notion leads to a methodological conception of 'competence' which we also regard as legitimate.

The competence-performance distinction is often conflated with the methodological distinction between an *underlying ability* of theoretical interest and *extraneous factors* that influence task performance. Because the tasks used in testing hypotheses about a specific ability are not pure assessments of that ability, it is appropriate and necessary to eliminate or vary extraneous factors that affect or mask the expression of the underlying ability. However, it should be noted that extraneous factors are extraneous only for the hypothesis being tested. They do not become theoretically uninteresting in general. Commonly cited 'performance' factors like memory, language comprehension, and cognitive style have significant developmental courses of their own. Memory abilities are 'performance' factors when reasoning

abilities are being investigated, but 'competence' when memory development is being investigated.

Confusion between Description and Explanation

The form of the competence-performance distinction which we find
objectionable was introduced by *Chomsky* [1965] to explicate the psychological relevance of his linguistic theory, and was first extended to Piagetian
theory by *Flavell and Wohlwill* [1969]. On *Chomsky's* conception, systematic
descriptive accounts of human task performances, known as 'competence
models', are wrongly presumed to have *explanatory* force in accounting for
how these performances are accomplished. [For a detailed analysis of *Chomsky's* position, see *Bickhard*, 1980b; *Bickhard and Campbell*, in preparation.]
Descriptive accounts of human capacities (such as grammars, rules, or
schemes) are classifications of possible human task performances. They
attempt to distinguish, within some task domain, tasks that can be successfully accomplished from those that cannot be, or judgments that will be made
from those that will not be, etc. Such descriptions have genuine theoretical
status, because they can be falsified by showing that some performance has
been misclassified. In many cases, such descriptions account for an infinite
domain of potential task accomplishments; in order to do so, they must use
recursive rules, or even more powerful functional languages (see Chapter 2).
Capacity descriptions attain to *descriptive adequacy* if they correctly classify
the possible performances.

What capacity descriptions cannot do, however, is *explain* how the performances they describe are accomplished. It is tempting to reify and inter-
nalize the capacity description, and make it part of the explanatory account.
Chomsky's [1965] conception of 'linguistic competence' is a capacity description (a grammar) which is to be reified and 'incorporated' into accounts of
language use and understanding. It has to be supplemented by a model of
'linguistic performance' that incorporates real-time psychological processes
in addition to the 'linguistic knowledge' supposedly described by the competence model. The claim that a capacity description or 'competence model'
describes internal representations commits a basic epistemological error: it
conflates a *description of what is known* with a *theory of knowing*. There cannot be a correspondence in detail (an isomorphism) between things that are
known and the means by which they are known. Assuming such an isomorphism is equivalent to positing foundational encodings, and is therefore incoherent – see Chapter 3.

In addition, there is not necessarily a correspondence between the boundaries of task domains and the boundaries of cognitive domains. The boundaries of domains of things known, assigned by the investigator, need not correspond to the internally emergent boundaries of domains of internal representation, or the boundaries of specialized knowing subsystems [*Campbell and Richie*, 1983; *Richie*, 1984]. *Chomsky* not only assumed domain correspondence, but claimed that knowledge of syntax was an autonomous mental faculty distinct from other human cognitive abilities [*Chomsky*, 1975; *Fodor*, 1983]. The sole basis for this claim was *Chomsky's* [1975] contention that syntax was an autonomous area of linguistic description because it had primitive concepts that were not derived from semantics or phonology. Because syntax was an autonomous domain of linguistic description, it was presumed to be understood by a special, encapsulated knowing subsystem independent of other cognitive systems [for additional problems with standard conceptions of syntax, see *Bickhard*, 1980b, in press; *Bickhard and Campbell*, in press].

The final reason that a capacity description, like *Chomsky's* model of linguistic competence, cannot be explanatorily adequate is that a theory of knowing is about processes, and the competence model contains no process concepts [*Bickhard*, 1980b]. This deficiency is sometimes overlooked, especially when capacity descriptions use recursive rules or functional languages that can make them sound like process models (see our discussion of the descriptive use of formal languages in Chapter 2). All that capacity descriptions can do is describe sets of possible human task performances. Although not explanatory models, they do constrain what kinds of explanatory models can be proposed, because any explanatory model must account for the described capacity.

Piagetian Structures and 'Competence Models'

Extending the Chomskyan competence-performance distinction to Piagetian theory was straightforward [*Flavell and Wohlwill*, 1969; *Broughton*, 1981a; *Overton and Newman*, 1982]. *Piaget's* structural stage models, such as the combinatorial and the INRC group, were treated as competence models. To account for actual performance on Piagetian tasks, the competence model was to be supplemented with a performance model, including memory, attention, task variations, etc.

Piagetian structuralism makes fundamental errors that encourage the application of the competence-performance distinction. As we have seen, *Piaget's* structural concepts (like schemes and operatory structures) really describe a range of task accomplishments. At the same time, however, structures are meant to be psychologically real and to explain how the tasks are accomplished. *Piaget* treated his operatory structures as though they described processes (internalized actions, transformations, closed systems), self-maintaining and self-regulating processes in fact (see Chapter 2). But his static algebraic formalisms for these structures contain no process concepts [*Bickhard*, 1980b, 1982].

The central error of structuralism is clearly expressed in *Inhelder and Piaget's* original treatment of formal operations. *Piaget* considered a description of possibilities (possible combinations to be tested, in the form of the combinatorial) to have explanatory force in accounting for which of the possibilities gets actualized (which combinations the reasoner actually tests in a particular situation). *Piaget* saw no need for an underlying mechanism or principle of emergence to explain the set of possibilities described. Structures, after all, were self-sufficient and ultimately explanatory: 'To be real, a structure must, in the literal sense, be governed from within' [*Piaget*, 1970a, p. 69]. In other words, *Piaget* conflated the systematic structural description of possible actions with an explanation of how particular actions occur. *Inhelder and Piaget* maintained that the algebraic group-lattice structure that they used to characterize formal thought constituted a set of structural possibilities. Some of these possibilities were actualized when the subject constructed particular operations or operational schemes. The remaining, unrealized possibilities took the form of potential transformations. Although the integrated structure consisted in part of 'simple possibilities' or unrealized transformations, 'the totality has causal efficacy, because... what is psychologically possible can orient what is actually constructed' [*Inhelder and Piaget*, 1955, pp. 293–294; cf. 1958, pp. 330–331].

A description of a set of possible actions cannot explain how any of those actions actually come to be done. Nor can it explain why just those actions (and no others) are possible. The set of possible operations cannot *cause* the operations actually carried out in a particular situation. A causal explanation, in terms of underlying processes, is needed, not just to account for the set of operations that could be carried out, but also to account for the operations that do get carried out in the appropriate circumstances. *Inhelder and Piaget*, however, considered the set of possible operations ('potential transformations') to have 'causal efficacy' all by itself. In fact, they expressly affirmed the sufficiency of structural description (as long as the structures had the right mathematical properties) for causal explanation. They claimed that the operations that the subject actually carried out were caused not only by prior thoughts and actions, but by the whole structural set of possible operations.

Inhelder and Piaget were at pains to distinguish their 'causality of the possible' from vacuous appeals to the Aristotelian act-potency distinction made by some Scholastic philosophers. Such maneuvers consisted of 'explaining' what a thing did (the 'act') by attributing to the thing a completely unanalyzed 'potency'. By contrast, 'what is genuinely potential ... can be described mathematically and meets the requirements of conserving the total system (as do potential transformations in physics)' [*Inhelder and Piaget*, 1955, p. 234; cf. 1958, pp. 265–266].

Inhelder and Piaget regarded a formal description of things the reasoner can do as an explanation of what the reasoner does. Moreover, the description of what can be done did not need to be grounded in any model of more fundamental properties of the reasoner: it was not necessary to ask what else about the reasoner enables him or her to do the things described. If the structural description had conservation and equilibrium properties, it was ipso facto self-regulating and explanatorily self-sufficient [cf. *Piaget*, 1970a, p. 14]. In fact, *Inhelder and Piaget's* appeal to the 'causality of the possible' is just as inadequate as the Scholastics' appeal to the act-potency distinction, and for the same reasons.

Piagetian structures, then, conflate descriptive and explanatory accounts in a manner typical of 'competence' models. Such conflations are also apparent in accounts like *Overton and Newman's* [1982] defense of Piagetian structures as competence models. Competence models are 'abstract systems of behavior potentialities' [p. 224], i.e., capacity descriptions. But they also describe 'the form ... of the individual's knowledge' [p. 218] and performance variables 'determine the application of competence in actual thought and behavior' [p. 222]. Now the competence models have become alleged descriptions of internal representations, which must be incorporated into an explanatory account.

The defense of Piagetian structures as competence models is unsatisfactory for the reasons already given. The structures cannot explain task performance because they do not describe process. All they are is descriptive accounts of behavioral capacities which, if descriptively adequate, will constrain a theory of process, because it must explain the pattern of task performance which they capture. It is not clear, however, that formal operational structures are even descriptively adequate; many of the critiques that we have cited challenge their ability to describe the range of accomplishments normally regarded as advanced reasoning [e.g., *Lunzer*, 1978; *Apostel*, 1982; *Kitchener and Kitchener*, 1981]. But even an alternative structural model with greater descriptive adequacy would not be a model of internal representation and should not be incorporated into a process model.

Distortions of Developmental Theory and Research

In addition to the basic conceptual errors entailed by treating *Piaget's* algebraic structures as Chomskyan competence models, this procedure introduces serious distortions into developmental research and theory evaluation. One of these distortions is the bifurcation of psychological models into two components. The competence component contains the reified structures or principles of the capacity description; the performance component contains 'the psychological processes along with task and situational factors that determine the application of competence' [*Overton and Newman*, 1982, p. 218]. Psychological processes and representations are permanently segregated into a 'competence' class and a 'performance' class. This segregation runs counter to the distinction between abilities of interest and extraneous factors that we made above, because on that conception any process or representation is 'competence' when it is being studied, and 'performance' otherwise. (*Greeno* et al. [1984] reject the permanent segregation and acknowledge that what is 'competence' and what is 'performance' varies with the ability of interest, although their conception is otherwise structural and Chomskyan.)

Accompanying the permanent segregation of competence and performance is the belief that competence is logically prior to performance. That is, the competence model is not to be constrained by considerations about cognitive or developmental processes, but the performance model which incorporates or applies competence is constrained by the competence model [*Chomsky*, 1975; *Overton and Newman*, 1982]. The assumption that competence is logically prior depends on the belief that descriptive models of capacity yield privileged access to internal representation. On a deeper level, it depends on the view that knowledge essentially consists of encoded representations, and that structural models disclose the encodings [on this epistemological error see Chapter 3; *Bickhard*, 1980b; *Bickhard and Richie*, 1983].

Another distortion produced by the competence-performance distinction is the dismissal of all conceptual criticism of the structural stage models. Apparent counterexamples to sequence and synchrony claims made by the structural model are always attributed to the interference of various performance factors. If a particular performance hypothesis fails to account for the anomaly, another performance hypothesis should be tried. In no case is the anomaly to be held against the competence model [*Overton and Newman*,

1982]. The appeal to performance hypotheses was intended as a response to empirical arguments [e.g., *Flavell*, 1977] that take empirical heterogeneities or asynchronies as a sufficient reason for rejecting structural stages. Under the influence of Lakatosian philosophy of science [*Lakatos*, 1978; *Overton*, 1984], however, it is tempting to treat the competence model as a theoretical 'hard core' which is held to be immune from refutation of any kind. As we pointed out in Chapter 2, Lakatosian philosophy of science seriously underestimates the role of conceptual criticism in theory evaluation [*Suppe*, 1977; *Laudan*, 1977]. In consequence, conceptual arguments against the structural model of formal operations are dismissed. A successful challenge to formal operations becomes inconceivable [*Tomlinson-Keasey*, 1982]. Formulations meant as alternatives to structural stage models are reduced to hypotheses about new performance factors, since no challenge to the structural model can be admitted. For instance, *Lunzer* [1978] proposed an alternative account of advanced reasoning that included acceptance of lack of closure. *Neimark* [1979] treated acceptance of lack of closure as a cognitive style variable that moderates formal operational competence, ignoring *Lunzer's* clear rejection of the structural model of formal operations.

A final distortion engendered by treating Piagetian structures as competence models is that developmental processes are relegated to second-class status. Because competence models implicitly presuppose an encoding conception of knowledge, and the encoding conception is antidevelopmental [Chapter 3; see also *Campbell and Bickhard*, 1985], this is a necessary consequence of the competence-performance distinction. The competence model consists of static structures or principles, not real-time processes. Developmental processes, like equilibration or reflective abstraction, must be part of the performance model. The only way to make equilibration part of the competence model is to reduce it to a static 'necessary' relation between the structures that describe successive stages [*Overton and Reese*, 1981]. It would reduce equilibration to a formal generator for a series of descriptive stages, as in *Commons and Richards'* [1984a, b] stage model. But this runs counter to all of *Piaget's* work on equilibration. Equilibration was never merely a formal generator for the structural stage sequence. It was meant to explain how cognitive change occurs and how new structures are constructed by the knower. Moreover, *Piaget* [1976, 1981] expressly denied that prior operatory structures were a sufficient basis for formal operations; practical problem-solving procedures were also prerequisites for formal operations, and procedures rather than operatory structures were the leading edge of development. The competence-performance distinction thus excludes developmental *processes* from the core of developmental theory, doing violence to *Piaget's* central insights and hindering theoretical progress.

In sum, it is not a valid defense of structural stage models, like *Piaget's* formal operations, to claim that they are competence models. The competence-performance distinction is based on a fundamental error, the conflation of descriptive accounts of what is known with explanatory accounts of how it is known. The use of the competence-performance distinction by some Piagetians has led to further distortions, notably the exclusion of developmental processes from the core of developmental theory. The study of development would greatly benefit if the competence-performance distinction were firmly rejected. We need to construct true process models of knowing, not reified capacity descriptions. We need to construct models of developmental stages that are constrained by and consistent with accounts of developmental processes, not in conflict with them. The knowing-level account of developmental stages does not treat capacity descriptions as explanatory, and it builds directly on an account of the process of stage transition.

Finally, if there is to be any progress in the study of development, we must reject the de facto prohibition on conceptual arguments that has been associated with the competence-performance distinction. Conceptual arguments are the only basis for evaluating a programmatic proposal, like our knowing-level conception of developmental stages. Moreover, even when the proposal has been implemented as an empirical research program, choosing between it and rival proposals about stages necessarily depends on conceptual arguments [*Laudan*, 1977; *Nickles*, 1980b].

Although the competence-performance distinction is a significant barrier to progress in developmental theorizing, it is hardly the only one. Before further extending our applications of the knowing-level approach, we need to address another type of standard conception about stages that obstructs the adoption of more fruitful alternatives.

Expected Properties of Structural Stages

Temporal Homogeneity

Both Piagetians and anti-Piagetians generally attribute properties to stages that follow only from the structural approach. From a structuralist standpoint, it might indeed be asked why stages derived from levels of knowing should be called 'stages' at all. *Flavell* [1982] construes 'stage' as referring to a strong temporal homogeneity in the child's thinking, whether that homogeneity be the result of overarching structures, common underlying abilities, etc. *Flavell* wants the term 'stage' to refer to 'horizontal structure' [*Wohlwill*, 1973], a quality of thinking that, in its ideal form, is 'constant, consistent, uniform, and homogeneous in its character, quality, and level of cognitive maturity across all tasks, situations, and cognitive domains' [*Flavell*, 1982, p. 6]. He proposes using the term 'sequence' for temporal consistencies in order of acquisition that do not show this 'stage-like' homogeneity.

Stages derived from the levels of knowing have no grounds for claiming anything like Piagetian structures of the whole. Nor do they have any other basis for postulating the general temporal homogeneity to which *Flavell* wishes to reserve the term 'stage'. The levels of knowing impose a necessary sequence of developmental steps across all possible domains, but do not impose any a priori temporal homogeneity among those steps. Within this model, developments in various domains can be wildly out of phase. On what alternative criterion, then, do the levels of knowing really yield stages, rather than just steps within a sequence?

Representational Homogeneity

There is an additional principle of organization in this model which, though not one that *Flavell* considers, justifies using the term 'stage'. There is a homogeneity among equivalent steps of development across domains which, while not necessarily the temporal homogeneity that *Flavell* demands, is in some ways a deeper form of homogeneity. Nor is it simply a homogeneity of formal task structure, which is what neo-Piagetians like *Fischer* and *Commons* (see below) attempt to put in the place of temporal homogeneity. Each knowing-level step across all domains shares with all of its corresponding steps a homogeneity of representational level, of the number of reflective abstractions it is removed from the external environment. This is a homogeneity of representational nature among steps of development, rather than a temporal homogeneity among instances of thought. The levels of knowing not only impose a sequence of steps on development, they also impose a representational coherence upon those steps. They are levels of *knowing*, not just levels of formal process.

The distinction between levels of formal process and levels of knowing is of central importance in evaluating stage models (see below). We use the term 'formal' in the sense of *Block* [1980a, b], *Field* [1981], *Searle* [1981], and others concerned with the functionalist approach to mean processes and relationships among processes that are sensitive only to the 'form' of representations, not to their representational content – as in a computer program operating on formal symbols in memory.

Hierarchies of Subroutines versus Hierarchies of Knowing Levels

Our position can be contrasted, for example, with the neo-Piagetian structural models of development proposed by *Fischer* [1980] and by *Commons and Richards* [1984a, b]. We will emphasize *Fischer's* model in our discussion. *Fischer* has presented his model with admirable clarity and simplicity, and stated his metatheoretical commitments explicitly (see also Chapter 7 below). In consequence, the limitations of the neo-Piagetian approach are particularly easy to recognize in his model. *Fischer* views development as the progressive construction of more and more complex skills via such transformations as differentiation and combination. Similarly, *Commons and Richards* view development as the hierarchical composition of actions operating on elements.

Fischer's approach attempts to avoid some of the pitfalls of Piagetian stage models. Stage development is gradual, rather than abrupt, and moves at different rates in different domains, rather than at a temporally homogeneous pace governed by structures of the whole. Moreover, the major stage boundaries in *Fischer's* model are, intriguingly, half a cycle off the Piagetian stage boundaries. The representational tier, levels 4 through 7, starts around age 4, during the standard preoperational period. The abstract tier, levels 7 through 10, starts during the standard concrete operational period. Despite these modifications, however, *Fischer's* model does not have any more theoretical resources to deal with development beyond those of standard structural approaches, and in a key respect it is actually weaker than *Piaget's* approach.

Because *Fischer's* model characterizes skills in terms of mappings and systems of mappings, that is, in terms of algebraic structures, albeit a somewhat different kind from *Piaget's,* it is vulnerable to all of our previous criticisms of structural stage models. Any computable mapping – a basic kind of skill for *Fischer* – is consistent with an unbounded number of possible systems for computing that mapping. Similarly, any action in *Commons and Richard's* model is just a mathematical relation between elements, and such relations can be computed by an unbounded number of possible systems. Questions can also be raised concerning the adequacy of skills, however themselves characterized, to characterize all of development (e.g., values). The critical point here, however, is that the relationships among skills in *Fischer's* model are strictly *formal.* At best, the relationships possible among his skills are essentially those possible among subroutines: they can call upon one another, they can coordinate or be coordinated within other routines, etc. Such formal relationships among control structures are of fundamental importance, and much of development consists of elaborating and constructing more and more sophisticated formal functional organizations. But *Fischer's* relationships are *strictly* formal: all skills operate on the environment, and there is no place for systems that operate on, that interact with, that *know* other systems. There are *only* formal functional relationships, there are no 'semantic' or intentional relationships – and no transformations by which such relationships could be constructed: there is nothing akin to reflective abstraction. In place of a hierarchy of knowing levels, there is a hierarchy of control, a hierarchy of layered subroutines all operating at knowing-level 1. On its own terms, then, *Fischer's* model addresses development *within* a level of knowing, but cannot address relationships among nor ascent through those levels.

In the *Commons and Richards* model, the principle of ascent through the stages is hierarchical composition of actions: relations at stage *n* take relations at stage *n-1* as their arguments. Relations at one stage become elements for relations at the next stage. Supposedly the generator that characterizes the relations between stages *n-1* and *n* is 'implicitly reflective because actions are applied back onto previous stage products. It is not explicitly reflective in the sense that stage change involves conscious reflection on previous thinking . . . [but] it is possible for the generator to become explicitly reflective' [*Commons and Richards*, 1984a, p. 124]. This claim cannot be sustained. The *Commons and Richards* stage model is isomorphic to *Fischer's* model. It contains no representation of knowing relationships between one level and another; in fact, the stage model is steadfastly task-descriptive, and so has no way to represent internal cognitive processes of any kind, let alone conscious processes.

A parallel critique of two other post-Piagetian structural stage models [*Pascual-Leone*, 1980; *Case*, 1978] has been made by *Kuhn* [1983]. *Pascual-Leone* and *Case* define stages in terms of a dimensional task analysis. There is a hierarchy of stages that depends on the dimensionality (the formal decomposition into subtasks) of the tasks that can be solved at each successive stage. The capacity to deal with added dimensions is reified as an ability called *M*-power, which is held to increase with age. *Kuhn* points out that although these stage theories admit an 'executive' that strings together the schemes needed to solve tasks, the executive resembles that found in strict information-processing accounts [e.g., *Kail and Bisanz*, 1982; *Sternberg and*

Powell, 1983]. An information-processing executive is essentially a high-level node in a decision tree, or a structure at the top of a hierarchy of control. The executive is not conscious and cannot abstract properties of the schemes, or examine them to see which is most appropriate for a given problem. In short, what is missing from these accounts is reflective abstraction. Like *Fischer's* [1980] stage theory, these 'neo-Piagetian' accounts acknowledge a hierarchy of control within a single knowing level, but not a hierarchy of levels of knowing, and hence are significantly weaker than *Piaget's* own account.

Indeed, a purely structural account of the development of formal operations [*Inhelder and Piaget*, 1958] has this same difficulty. If formal operations develop simply by consolidating and integrating the algebraic structures of concrete operations into one big algebraic structure, this is purely a within-knowing-level process, without reflection or knowing-level ascension [cf. *Blasi and Hoeffel*, 1974]. The constructive process of reflective abstraction has to be introduced in order to capture knowing-level differences between concrete and formal operations. Piagetian structures as such have only formal functional relations between them. *Piaget* [1976, 1977b, 1981] later realized the inadequacy of a purely structural account of the development of formal operations (see below).

Inadequate Power of Subroutine Hierarchy Models

Two points of interesting comparison to *Fischer's* model and to *Commons and Richard's* model are provided by *Powers* [1973] and *Cunningham* [1972]. In *Powers'* model, behavior is viewed as being controlled not by mappings as in *Fischer's* model, but by feedback-controlled servomechanisms. The conceptual focus of *Powers'* model, in fact, is that behavior is always for the sake of controlling perception – that is, is regulated by feedback from the environment. *Powers* begins with an analysis of the low-level neural control of behavior and builds a model of a hierarchy of servomechanisms, each level of which regulates a higher level of representation of reality and concomitant mental activity. The hierarchy terminates with somewhat tentative explications of cognitive relationships and behavioral principles.

Cunningham's model is an attempt to explicate the steps of development through the substages of *Piaget's* sensory-motor period in terms of progressive coordinations of Hebbian cell assemblies. The principles used in this lower-level model are extended more speculatively to account for higher-level activity such as conceptual thought and language.

Both models have in common with *Fischer's* and *Commons'* models a restriction to strictly formal control-system relationships, with nothing akin to a hierarchy of knowing levels – there are no epistemic reflections or iterations. Thus the hierarchies in all four models are essentially layers of subroutines. They are all models of the same basic type, and the differences among them are revealing of some of the basic issues involved in such modeling.

One immediate point of comparison is that *Powers'* model makes extensive and foundational use of the concept of feedback, while *Fischer's* does not. The power of feedback systems over straight mappings is clear intuitively, mathematically, and in terms of the reality of neural functioning. What is not clear is how *Fischer* can claim to account for phenomena, even very low level phenomena, that *Powers* explicates in terms of feedback, with a model that does not acknowledge or even allow it. *Fischer's* mappings (and *Commons'* 'actions') are simply too weak as a presumed process language to be able to account for much of the ontology of what actually takes place, either synchronically or diachronically.

A still deeper comparison, however, derives from the fact that the four models use varying numbers of subroutine layers to get from their base level to comparable levels of explication. *Powers* uses five levels to get to the control of sequence in behavior, eight to account for control of principles, and nine for control of system concepts. *Cunningham* requires six to get out of the sensory-motor period, and then appeals to increases in short-term memory units (as in *Pascual-Leone's* model) to account for further development. *Fischer* postulates ten levels to account for such skills as higher forms of arithmetic understanding [*Fischer* et al., 1984]. *Commons and Richards* posit seven stages to account for unified field theories. What this diversity indicates is not that any particular one of these models is necessarily wrong, but rather that *all* subroutine hierarchy models are largely arbitrary.

There are no natural or intrinsic direct divisions between levels or layers of subroutines: one model may use three layers where another uses one, while a third may not have *any* boundaries of layers in common with the first two, and a fourth may aim the hierarchy in a completely different direction – and there might well be no intrinsic basis for deciding against any of them. For instance, *Fischer* posits within each 'tier' of development four recurring levels, based on increasingly complex types of mappings. These are (1) simple skills or representational units; (2) unidirectional mappings from one unit to another; (3) bidirectional mappings of units, and (4) bidirectional mappings of bidirectional mappings of units. Other levels are imaginable and equally plausible, e.g. (3a) unidirectional mappings from one bidirectional mapping to another, but they are excluded from the model without argument.

The division of a task into a hierarchy of subtasks can be done in an infinite number of ways, so claims concerning the psychological and developmental reality of any particular subtask hierarchy must be based upon additional explicit criteria beyond prima facie plausibility. It might be added that information processing approaches to development that avoid positing stages [e.g., *Siegler*, 1981; *Kail and Bisanz*, 1982] prefer to explain development in terms of the coordination of preexisting abilities (i.e., the coordination of subtasks), and are thus also vulnerable to the arbitrariness of freely chosen subtask analyses.

An additional source of arbitrariness in such models derives from their reliance on a concept of representational elements or units. The layers of subroutines are presumed to operate with or upon such elements. *Cunningham* has representational and memory unit 'elements'; *Powers* has reference 'signals' for his servomechanisms; *Fischer* maps representational 'elements' or 'sets' into one another; *Commons and Richards* have actions or relations which coordinate 'elements', and so on. The arbitrariness derives from the fact that such elements are largely ad hoc units of analysis. *Powers'* lowest level elements are involved in the muscle spindle receptor controls of muscular contractions; *Cunningham's, Fischer's,* and *Commons and Richards'* elements begin at a higher level – this initial arbitrariness concerning what constitutes the lowest level is fairly obvious, but the principle(s) involved in the movement up the hierarchy are equally arbitrary, if not more so. The movement from one level of elements to the next generally constitutes a movement to a higher level of representation, but, since representation has not been explicated, what goes into this next level of representation is a matter of intuitive appeal rather than explicit analysis and explication. In fact, such representational elements or units are encodings, and are therefore vulnerable to all of the critical arguments of Chapter 3.

The deficiencies and ad hocness of subroutine-hierarchy approaches are particularly apparent when the posited movement to a new level of subroutines and elements in fact involves epistemic reflection – something that subroutine control flow relationships cannot *possibly* explicate on their own. *Fischer's* model begins at the lowest tier with skill units or 'sensory-motor sets' that already presume an (unspecified) analysis of perception and basic action systems; sufficiently complex mappings of such units yield 'representational sets' at the next tier; sufficiently complex mappings of those units in turn yield 'abstract sets' at the next tier. An issue that clearly involves epistemic reflection is the development of the ability to explicitly define the relations between addition, subtraction, multiplication, and division in terms of inversion and iteration [e.g., *Fischer* et al., 1984]. In *Fischer's* model this transition must be treated as a move from the representational tier to the abstract tier. The model does not permit explicit references to consciousness, so the knowing level ascension must be smuggled into the change of units. Moreover, the relations between mathematical operations to be understood must be distorted to fit the 4 sublevels with their arbitrarily chosen layers of mappings. The higher stages for *Richards and Commons* [1984] involve explicitly representing mathematical systems and extracting their properties, and stage ascension is considered analogous to ascending from logic to meta-logic. But the stage model can only account for such ascensions by positing relations operating on elements at the prior stage. Such representational elements are the neofunctionalist's equivalents, and often the historical descendents, of the behaviorist's S's and R's: anything that the model has trouble explicating can be buried in them. The fundamental inadequacies of the approach to modeling are thus shoved out of sight – and too often out of mind.

The Structuralist's Dilemma

In addition to the problems that beset a strictly formalist approach to stages, there are deep connections between formalist and structuralist stage conceptions. Any model which takes into account only formal relationships may by definition only have recourse to formal principles of structure and homogeneity [cf. *Fodor*, 1981, and *Bickhard and Richie*, 1983]. The only way that such an approach can introduce and account for structure in the mind, then, is by appealing to such formal structural principles. In such a view, more (deeper) explanation is naturally construed as more structure. But more *structure* cannot be the equivalent of more *structures:* the extreme of that direction is a separate structure for each behavior, and that is *no* structure at all. 'As the number of task specific competence models [i.e., structures] increase, theoretical power decreases' [*Overton and Newman*, 1982, p. 225; cf. *Turiel and Davidson*, 1985]. Rather, *more structure* must be broader and broader scope for *fewer structures*. The extreme of that direction is to posit single overarching structures with (essentially) universal scope. Such pervasive scope necessarily implies massive temporal homogeneity [*Flavell*, 1982], and abrupt, discontinuous transitions between structural stages. Or it requires elaborate competence-performance epicycles [as in *Overton and Newman*, 1982] to deal with the heterogeneous task accomplishments actually observed.

The fact that global temporal homogeneities do not exist has prompted many to abandon structurally universal stages in favor of sequences of smaller scale homogeneities – sequences within more restricted domains. This progression from global to local stage models is perfectly reasonable within its own perspective, but it neglects the possibility of representationally based principles of coherence and properties of development. Moreover, local stage models are no better than their definitions of psychological domains, and even the best of these models [e.g., *Turiel and Davidson,* 1985] fail to make an adequate distinction between psychological domains for the knower and task domains defined by the investigator [*Richie,* 1984].

We have argued that the expectation, grounded in formalist and structuralist conceptions, that stages be temporally homogeneous across domains is neither reasonable nor necessary. There are other principles of coherence that hold across sequences in different developmental domains and that could be used to define developmental stages. Whether or not the coherences (among corresponding steps of development across various domains) that are imposed by the levels of knowing are to be called 'stages' is ultimately, of course, a matter of definition and consensual usage, but they are surely something more than just vast collections of sequences of steps of disparate formal homogeneities within atomized domains.

Conclusion: Knowing-Level Stages versus Structural Stages

The hierarchy of knowing levels generated by iterating the knowing relationship provides a better foundation for developmental stages than does the current structural approach. Specifically, we have contrasted knowing-level 3 with Piagetian formal operations. Knowing-level stages are defined in terms of a hierarchy of levels of knowing, and are applicable to sequences in any developmental domain; they are not restricted to particular structures or contents. Knowing levels are part of a theoretical framework that seeks explanations of cognitive processes and is not limited to descriptive analyses of problems that can be solved. Knowing-level stages are homogeneous in terms of representational level without having to be temporally homogeneous; the integrity or coherence of a knowing-level stage is not violated because the same stage is attained in different domains at different times. Knowing-level stages are marked by the initial emergence of new abilities at the higher level, not the construction of invariants or algorithms, or the final systematic integration of abilities at the new level. Finally, knowing levels are defined in terms of developmental processes, specifically in terms of reflective abstraction, the process by which properties of the representations in one knowing level are abstracted at the next level.

The key properties of knowing-level stages are quite different from the key properties of structural stages like *Piaget's* formal operations. Structural stages are defined in terms of algebraic structures. Such structures are descriptive logical analyses of successful performance on classes of tasks. In consequence, the structural analyses are specific to certain task domains and cannot be readily generalized to other domains. Moreover, the structures say nothing about cognitive processes; they cannot explain how the tasks are solved. Structural stages are expected to be temporally homogeneous (to have 'horizontal structure'); tasks that are given the same structural analysis should be solved about the same time. Structural stages are marked by the acquisition of systematic algorithms, or invariance representations, or equilibrated systems of representations; the origins of such representations, if noted at all, are relegated to a prior 'transitional' substage. In the extreme case, temporal homogeneity and the emphasis on already integrated systems are combined to yield structures of the whole as definitive of stages. Structurally-defined stages are not based on accounts of developmental processes. In some cases [e.g., *Overton and Newman*, 1982] structural stage theories lead to a lack of interest in developmental processes. In other cases [e.g., *Fischer*, 1980] they lead to an impoverished account which acknowledges processes of learning within knowing levels, but not reflective abstraction or knowing-level ascension. *Piaget* [e.g., 1977a] did acknowledge reflective abstraction, and considered it of central importance, but, as we will show in Chapter 5, his account of reflective abstraction clashed with his own structural account of stages.

Defenders of structural stages [e.g., *Overton and Newman*, 1982; *Tomlinson-Keasey*, 1982] tend to regard critiques of structural stages as rejections of the explanatory value of stages per se. It should be clear from our presentation of the knowing-levels model that our critique fully acknowledges the explanatory value of developmental stages. In fact, we would argue that the structuralists do not fully appreciate the explanatory significance of stages (see Chapter 2). The rejection of stage explanations per se is commonly a holdover from logical positivist philosophy of science, based on the restriction of valid explanations to antecedent-consequent, efficient causal explanations [see *Bickhard* et al., 1985, for a detailed examination of a positivistic attack on stages].

We have emphasized the need for an approach to stages that recognizes stages as intrinsic constraints on development, and characterizes constraints on development in terms of developmental processes. An issue that cuts even deeper than how stages are defined is what developmental processes are recognized in the first place. The knowing-levels model depends on the recognition of a metaprocess of reflective knowing or reflective abstraction. In contrasting the knowing-level approach with *Piaget's* structuralism, we have focused our critique on a stage model that recognizes reflective abstraction. However, there are other models of development that do not recognize reflective abstraction at all. The denial of reflective abstraction is certainly characteristic of anticonstructivist and information-processing models. But it is also characteristic of structural stage models like those of *Case* [1978], *Pascual-Leone* [1980], *Fischer* [1980], and *Commons and Richards* [1984a], which recognize control and information flow relationships, but not epistemic or knowing-level relationships in development. As *Kuhn* [1983] has argued, the fundamental question of the existence of reflective abstraction, or of a 'meaning-making executive' that considers other aspects of the knowing system, divides *Piaget's* constructivist approach to development from virtually all of the others now prevalent.

It remains, however, for us to present a detailed explication of the process of reflective abstraction in terms of the knowing-levels model. This will be a major aim of Chapter 5. We will also review *Piaget's* [1976, 1977b] most explicit and advanced treatment of reflective abstraction, in his discussion of the development of logical necessity, and show how his process account of the development of necessity clashed with his prior position that necessity was a property of algebraic structures like the concrete operational groupings.

In Chapter 6, we will illustrate this conflict between process and structural accounts of necessity by showing how the transition from an implicit to an explicit understanding of logical necessity has proven anomalous for the Piagetian structural stage model, but is readily explained in terms of the knowing-levels model. In Chapter 7, we will examine the implications of the knowing-levels model for the development of 'postformal' stages, including the possibility of stages beyond the simply ordered, linear sequence of knowing levels. Finally, in Chapter 8, we will illustrate the generality of the knowing levels approach by sketching an account of the development of values, the self, and identity in terms of the knowing levels.

5. Reflective Abstraction

In Chapter 4 we presented a new approach to developmental stages. Our approach derives stages from the sequence of levels of knowing generated by a reflective iteration of the basic knowing relationship [*Bickhard,* 1978, 1980a]. Knowing-level stages have quite different properties from Piagetian stages, which are defined in terms of algebraic structures. In general, knowing-level stages are directly grounded in considerations about developmental processes, whereas structural stages are not. We illustrated the differences between knowing levels and structural stages by contrasting knowing level 3 with the structural account of formal operations [*Inhelder and Piaget,* 1958]. We showed that *Piaget's* algebraic structures can at best describe solutions to classes of tasks, but not explain how people solve the tasks. Moreover, the structures cannot be readily generalized to other developmental domains. The attempt to defend structural stages as models of 'competence' rather than 'performance' perpetuates the confusion between describing potential task accomplishments and explaining how the accomplishments are done. It also leads to a loss of interest in developmental processes. We criticized other assumptions about stages that derive from the structural approach, such as the expectation that stages be temporally homogeneous; knowing-level stages are representationally homogeneous without being temporally homogeneous.

A major outcome of our examination of structural stage models in Chapter 4 was that the presence or absence of knowing-level ascension, or reflective abstraction, is a major issue in developmental theories [cf. *Kuhn,* 1983]. Not only anticonstructivist and information-processing theories of development, but also many structural stage theories, fail to recognize reflective abstraction as a process. *Piaget* attempted to combine reflective abstraction with structural stages. Our aim here is to explicate the process of reflective abstraction in terms of the knowing-levels model. We contrast reflective abstraction with the supposedly related conceptions of metacognition and accessing. We also examine *Piaget's* [1976, 1977b] account of the development of logical necessity through reflective abstraction, and show how the make individual and cultural ascent through new levels impossible. Whether or not there is more than one physical knowing level, there must be some strictly functional way to ascend the levels of knowing.

Suppose that a system could learn to create external indicators of various points in and aspects of its own internal processes – as it was actually engaged in those processes. Then the indicators would manifest properties of the organization and functioning of those internal processes. Being external, the indicators would be available for examination by the system itself. From the indicators, the system could then abstract properties of the processes that yielded those indicators. That is, using such indicators, a system could reflectively abstract its own properties. A knowing system with such a resource of external indicators, then, would be capable of a functional reflective abstraction ascending through the levels of knowing. The basic process is an externalization of steps and aspects of internal processing (reflection), followed by the construction of knowing subsystems for properties inherent in those external indicators (abstraction). Most likely there would be multiple iterations of these two phases.

Whether reflective abstraction is possible is thus now reduced to whether such a resource of external indicators is possible. *Bickhard* [1980a] argues that an adequate system of such indicators cannot be expected to develop or evolve unless those indicators are true symbols (otherwise they will not have a sufficient range of usefulness to encounter a smooth trajectory of selection pressures) and that true symbols are impossible except in a species that already has two physical knowing-level systems. With only one knowing level, external events and entities can only be reacted to. They cannot be considered in virtue of their meaning (which involves level two knowing level one). 'Fire', if it existed in any form, would only have the same impact as the smell of smoke. An example would be a danger call in a herd animal: it is a signal, a substitute, for the sight or sound or smell of danger, but it cannot be treated as a symbol. *Bickhard* [1980a] also examines a plausible evolutionary trajectory (knowing, learning, emotions, and consciousness) and corresponding selection pressures that could yield such a physical second knowing level system (see Chapter 3). Under this analysis, reflective abstraction requires *both* an initial two-physical-level knowing system (a knowing system with consciousness) *and* a subsequent two-phase functional process to ascend through higher levels of knowing.

Basically, the two-physical-level system is required for the evolution and development of symbolic language (or some equivalent examinable system of representational indicators), and language is required for the possibility of the functional ascent, the reflective abstraction, through higher levels of knowing. Although we cannot pursue it here, we have arrived at a model of the interplay and interdependence of thought and language, and of language and development, that does not reduce either one to the other. Furthermore, with language as the primary means by which the child contacts his or her society and culture, and with language as an essential aspect of development beyond knowing level 1, we also have a perspective on the essential constitutive and developmental role of society and culture in the development of the child, again without reducing either side to the other – in this case, without reducing the child, the person, to a mere nexus or intersection point of cultural and social meanings and activities, and, conversely, without reducing society to a mere collection of autonomously constructed and constituted individuals (see also our comments on hermeneutics in Chapter 8). Further pursuit of these directions requires a model of language, of the social level of reality, and of the relations between the two [see *Bickhard*, 1980b; in press].

Reflective Abstraction in the Development of Logic

The process of reflective abstraction can be illustrated historically by *Aristotle's* formalization of syllogistic logic (a possible developmental parallel is provided by *Moshman and Franks'* [in press] work on the abstraction of logical form and inferential validity). In examining many arguments (reflection), *Aristotle* began using single letters as abbreviations. At some point, these abbreviations became variables within a general form (abstraction) [*Bochenski*, 1970]. This example is in a powerful sense paradigmatic, since to abstract a class of variables is ipso facto to abstract the framework within which they *are* variables. It also illustrates how an external medium of symbolic representation, usually language, is essential. Finally, it is an apt example in that understanding of the logical necessity of an argument, such as a syllogism, is a knowing-level-3 accomplishment – an accomplishment that is at best presupposed in the definition of formal operations, but can be explained within the knowing levels model. (*Aristotle's* brilliant discovery of how to *formalize* that logical necessity, however, requires at least level 4.)

A parallel case that obviously involves the abstraction of variables is the development of algebra out of arithmetic: 'reflective abstraction is the general constructive process of mathematics; it has served, for example, to evolve algebra out of arithmetic, as a set of operations on operations' [*Piaget*, 1970b, p. 728].

A possible developmental example of reflective abstraction by means of external indicators that serve as variables is provided by *Voelin's* [1976] work on higher-level class-inclusion reasoning. After presenting a standard class-inclusion problem, the experimenter asked, 'Is there a way to make it so we have more yellow flowers than flowers in front of us?' If children said there was a way, the experimenter asked them to demonstrate how. Several children explored possible transformations and ended up realizing that there was no way to modify the inclusion relationship. They 'took away the flowers of other colors, and noticed that there were "the same number" [of flowers and yellow flowers]. Then they proposed adding a lot of yellow flowers, and realized that each yellow flower also counted as a flower. It was at this moment that they realized that there was nothing that could be done to have more yellow flowers than flowers' [*Voelin*, 1976, p. 277]. This may be a concrete example of how reflective abstraction proceeds. We do not know whether these children would have generalized their conclusion to other instances of the class-inclusion relationship. In any case, their procedure was not 'merely empirical': they selected only quantity-relevant transformations (adding to the subclass, subtracting from the superordinate class) for examination. Moreover, they tried just one or two instances of each type. To conclude that the inclusion relationship could not be reversed they had to generalize over transformations, since an indefinite number of untried transformations remained.

Reflective Abstraction versus Metacognition and Accessing

Metacognition

Our account of reflective abstraction as a process permits us to differentiate reflective abstraction from the supposedly related concepts of metacognition and accessing. On the face of it, *metacognition* (knowledge about constraints on knowing processes) should be regarded as a specific type of higher-level knowledge, based on reflective abstraction. With the exception of *Flavell and Wellman* [1977], however, researchers have made no attempt to treat metacognitive understanding as a product of reflective abstraction. In part, this is because no interest has been shown in how metacognitive abilities develop [*Cavanaugh and Perlmutter*, 1982]. Moreover, work on metacognition usually employs an information-processing approach, in which knowing-level distinctions are not made. Metacognition is just a label on another box in the information-processing boxology. Sometimes this box is called an 'executive' or a 'metacomponent' [*Sternberg and Powell*, 1983]. In a typical information-processing definition, '*Metacognition* refers to cognitions about cognitions or the executive decision-making process in which the individual must both carry out cognitive operations and oversee his or her progress' [*Meichenbaum* et al., 1985, p. 5]. An information-processing executive does not examine or consider other information-processing abilities; a metacomponent controls 'components', but it does not know them. An information-processing executive is simply the highest level of control in a subroutine hierarchy, and it lacks any property of reflective consciousness. It is not a 'meaning-making executive' [*Kuhn*, 1983].

When a concept that makes reference to knowing levels or to reflective consciousness is inserted into a theory that does not recognize these things, conceptual problems are bound to follow. Work on metamemory suffers not only from the weakness of theory about memory abilities as such, but also from the lack of a clear conception of how metamemory relates to memory abilities [*Cavanaugh and Perlmutter*, 1982]. Discussions of metalinguistic abilities frequently confuse reflection on properties of language with undirected playful variations and error-correction procedures, which are part of the basic language learning process [*Hakes*, 1982]. In general, metacognition is not distinguished from learning. 'Confused in the metacognitive literature, even lost in some versions of the concept, is this essential distinction between self-regulation during learning and knowledge of, or even mental experimentation with, one's own thoughts. Whatever distinctions must be made to render metacognition a more malleable concept, this one is a fine candidate for inclusion in the list' [*Brown* et al., 1983, p. 122]. The distinction is even more fundamental than *Brown* suggests. Unless the essential connection between knowing levels and metacognition becomes clearly understood, metacognition will continue to be trivialized.

Accessing

While metacognition requires reference to knowing levels, but is usually inserted into nonknowing-level theories, *accessing* is a thoroughly nonknowing-level conception that has been used as a surrogate for reflective abstraction. Although *Brown* [1982] carefully distinguishes accessing from metacognition, this distinction is usually blurred by others [e.g., *Mandler*, 1983]. The notion of accessing was introduced by *Rozin* [1976]. The root metaphor behind accessing is connecting previously isolated subcomponents, or mental faculties, and passing information between them; in *Rozin's* examples, this is often thought to involve actual neural connections between different parts of the brain that serve localized functions. Most of these examples are cases of generalizing the application of previously specialized abilities. Such generalizations or extensions of prior knowledge are typical of development within a knowing level. *Rozin* also discusses cases in which there is reflection on a specialized ability, and some implicit property of that ability is made explicit, which he calls 'accessing to consciousness'. From his standpoint, there is no difference between accessing to consciousness and accessing to any other subcomponent, between reflection and generalization without reflection. That is, no basic difference is recognized between learning within a level of knowing, and ascending to the next level of knowing.

Like structural stage theories without reflective abstraction [e.g., *Fischer,* 1980], a theory of development that posits accessing as the basic developmental process acknowledges a hierarchy of subroutines, but not a hierarchy of knowing levels. It presents an account of development in terms of formal processes, but not in terms of the 'semantic' relations between the knowing system and what it knows. Whereas theorists like *Fischer* do attempt to specify the types of 'transformations' that build more complex skills, or mappings, out of less complex ones, accessing remains completely unspecified. (In fact, *Rozin's* conception of connections between specialized parts of the brain is no more powerful than strict associationism.) Accessing is a concept based on a fundamental confusion, between learning within a knowing level and ascent between knowing levels, and it should be avoided in developmental theorizing. Its current appeal to some theorists [e.g., *Gelman,* 1982] is that it appears to do the work of reflective abstraction [*Greeno* et al., 1984, actively conflate accessing with reflective abstraction], while satisfying anticonstructivist strictures against the emergence of genuine novelty and, especially, against any growth in logical power through development [e.g., *Fodor,* 1972]. The formal interactive basis for the knowing levels model [*Bickhard,* 1980a; *Campbell and Bickhard,* 1985] reveals that such strictures are groundless; it shows how ascent through the levels and increases in logical power are possible, and in fact must be recognized in cognitive development.

Piaget on Reflective Abstraction and Logical Necessity

Process versus Structure
Piaget's [1976, 1977b] account of the development of logical necessity includes his clearest description of reflective abstraction, though in terms of the role that reflective abstraction plays in the development of necessity, not the details of the process. It also illustrates the tension in *Piaget's* theory

between structurally defined stages and reflective abstraction as a process of transition between them.

Piaget's earlier conceptions of reflective abstraction subordinated it entirely to his structural stage models: reflective abstraction was what got the child from one structurally defined stage to the next. *Piaget's* [1970b] account emphasized the metaphor of 'reflection onto a higher plane' when discussing reflective abstraction; the 'higher plane' was not characterized in terms of the process that produces it, but rather in terms of the structural stage model. It almost seemed as though the structures must already be there. At this point, reflective abstraction was an appendage to the structural model that was used to account for the origins of novel logicomathematical structures. It was when *Piaget* [1975, 1978, 1981, 1983] became concerned about consciousness, about equilibration and other constructive processes, and about necessity and possibility, that reflective abstraction became a process in its own right.

A disclaimer is in order concerning one feature of *Piaget's* account of logical necessity. Consistent with his conception of causality as a mathematicized functional relation between events, *Piaget* [1977b] attempted to reduce causal necessity to logical necessity. As *Harré, Wallace,* and other philosophers of science have shown (see Chapter 2), causal necessity must have an ontological basis, and cannot be assimilated to logical necessity. We have also shown that *Inhelder and Piaget's* structural model of formal operations is incapable of describing causal reasoning (Chapter 4). In consequence, we do not consider *Piaget's* account of logical necessity to be an account of the development of causal necessity.

From the standpoint of process, *Piaget* [1977b, 1981, 1983] held that logical necessities were understood as a result of generating various possibilities (a process of differentiation) and recognizing properties that hold across all of the relevant possibilities (a process of integration). Generating the relevant possibilities requires actual procedures for solving problems, or 'procedural schemes', not just operatory structures. An understanding of necessity involves taking possibilities which were 'extrinsic variations' to be observed or interacted with, and representing and anticipating them as 'intrinsic variations' that can be deduced within a closed system. Constructing the closed system of intrinsic variations requires reflective abstraction. It involves finding and representing the reason for the variations, or some common property that holds across the variations. Such reasons and properties were already implicit in the representational system, but had to be reflectively abstracted from it.

There is a strong resemblance between *Piaget's* process account of logical necessity and the account produced by the knowing-levels approach. On the knowing-levels approach, necessity is a property of relations between representations. Logical necessity involves *epistemic exhaustiveness.* It requires an exhaustive determination concerning all of the relevant possible alternatives. In a finite domain, each alternative can be inspected in order to determine whether a property holds across all of them. In an infinite domain, such a 'trivial' inspection process is no longer possible. What can be done is to use an interactive procedure as an implicit definition of that infinite domain. (An interactive procedure can be said to implicitly define the class of aspects of its environment that 'fit' it or can be successfully assimilated to it [*Bickhard,* 1980b; 1982]; see Chapter 3 above.) However, this requires interacting with the procedure, moving from considering various instances of the implicitly defined class to considering the *implicit form* of that procedure; i.e., to considering the properties of the procedure that are essential to its implicit definitional power. Interacting with the procedure to abstract its implicit form is reflective abstraction. Coming to know the property of logical necessity of a prior relation between implicitly defining representations requires principles of inference in order to draw the implications of the implicit definitions. Such principles of inference support conclusions of the form: 'Whatever meets this implicit definition *must* have these other (implicitly defined) properties.' In consequence, necessity at a given knowing level is relative to implicit assumptions that can only be examined at higher knowing levels [cf. *Moshman and Timmons,* 1982].

There are a number of obvious parallels between *Piaget's* process account of the development of necessity and the knowing-levels account. On the knowing-levels account, interactive procedures implicitly define an infinite domain, or class of possibilities, and reflective abstraction yields the implicit form of the procedure. In *Piaget's* account, it is reflective abstraction on signifying implications that yields a recognition of their necessity; signifying implications are implicative relations between schemes, including procedural schemes. In interactive terms, a signifying implication is just an implicative relation between interactive procedures. Moreover, the move from instances of the implicitly defined class to the implicit form corresponds to *Piaget's* move from extrinsic variations to intrinsic variations. Finally, the need for principles of inference corresponds to *Piaget's* requirement that necessity involve deduction 'in a non-extensional manner' (see below).

Epistemic Exhaustiveness versus Structural Closure

From the structural standpoint, however, *Piaget* continued to maintain that logical necessity was a property of algebraic structures, like the groupings of concrete operations and the group-lattice structure of formal operations. Necessity involves epistemic exhaustiveness: all of the relevant variations or kinds of possibilities have already been represented, and a determination has been made concerning all of these classes of possibilities, without requiring further empirical investigation. The assimilation of logical necessity to properties of algebraic structures depended on a key conflation between epistemic exhaustiveness (the ability to represent all of the relevant kinds of possibilities) and structural closure. To add to the confusion, *Piaget* also conflated *closed structures* and *closed systems*.

It is not possible to capture epistemic exhaustiveness in terms of properties of structures. As we showed in Chapter 4, structures cannot model properties of the knower because they are static and therefore inadequate to model cognitive processes. Even if we ignore the difficulty that structures are static, the best that can be obtained from structures is *structural exhaustiveness*. A structurally exhaustive description is one that correctly applies to all relevant classes of possible task accomplishments – the structural description is exhaustively applicable (applicable everywhere) within its range of relevance. The comprehensiveness and reversibility of Piagetian equilibrium states are instances of structural exhaustiveness over a wide range of task accomplishments. An example of structural exhaustiveness would be the fact that in all possible class-inclusion tasks, the extension of the class is always greater than or equal to the extension of any of its subclasses. The problem with structural exhaustiveness as a basis for logical necessity is that structural exhaustiveness is a descriptive concept. It describes an aspect of a space of potential task accomplishments, regardless of whether the knower can represent those possibilities – at best it captures something implicit in the knower's representation. It does not explain how (or whether) the knower represents those possibilities. In accounting for logical necessity, however, what is crucial is the classes of possibilities that the knower can represent. In fact, the properties of procedures that can be applied to an infinite domain (e.g., class-inclusion inferences, or counting procedures) cannot be known without reflecting on the procedures, without ascending to the next knowing level. So characterizing logical necessity in terms of structural exhaustiveness ignores knowing-level distinctions and makes it impossible to distinguish relationships between procedures that are implicitly necessary from explicit knowledge of their necessity.

Although structural exhaustiveness is clearly not an adequate substitute for epistemic exhaustiveness, it is worth noting that *Piaget's* structural account of necessity did not even appeal directly to structural exhaustiveness. Instead, structural exhaustiveness was assimilated to *structural closure*. An algebraic structure is closed if any operation maps an element or elements of the domain onto another element of that same domain. Structural closure is just not the same property as structural exhaustiveness. For instance, the concrete operational grouping that *Piaget* [1972a] used to describe class inclusion is closed because the result of 'adding' (or performing a set union operation on) any two classes is another class. There is no connection between the fact that this grouping is closed and the fact that in all cases the extension of the class is greater than or equal to the extension of any of its subclasses. Nor is there any connection between closure and necessity in general. If we take the positive and negative integers as our domain, addition and subtraction form a closed group structure and taking square roots does not form a closed group structure. It does not follow from this that the result of taking a square root is any less mathematically necessary than the result of adding or subtracting.

Piaget's [1971] interest in biology and systems theory led to an additional conflation, between closed structures and *closed systems*. This conflation was encouraged by *Piaget's* [1970a] tendency to attribute biological properties of self-regulation to structures: 'Even as a biological organism is viewed as a totality whose parts are integrated into a hierarchical whole, so structures are seen as biological wholes, with a dynamic as well as a static aspect to them' [*Gardner*, 1973, p. 172]. Systems, being dynamic rather than static, have an explanatory advantage over algebraic structures. However, the closure of a system, which consists in its being self-sufficient and isolated from the environment, has at best a metaphorical relationship to epistemic exhaustiveness. If taken as a serious model of the development of logical necessity, it produces immediate difficulties because the knower, in interaction with the environment, is surely an open system. The best psychological approximation to a closed system – one isolated from all new information – would be a self-protective pathological rigidity [*Bickhard*, 1985, in preparation]. Further confusions are introduced by treating closed structures as adequate models of closed systems. Closed structures are inadequate to model closed systems, not only because systems are dynamic and structures are static, but because the 'closure' properties are different. Nonetheless, *Piaget* [1976, 1977b] persisted in this equivocation about closure, and equated the strength and richness of a system of necessities with the power of the supposedly corresponding algebraic structure.

There are motivations for *Piaget's* conflations: an 'equilibrated system' is a 'closed structure' in the sense that all necessary accommodations are already present – closed with respect to accommodations. So, if such a structure were epistemically fundamental, then a closed such structure might seem to be epistemically exhaustive (all new knowledge, all new accommodations, are already included). Hence, anything true of every part of such a structure would therefore be exhaustively, necessarily, true. This line of thinking takes structures, not processes, as epistemically fundamental; it conflates properties true of a structure with knowledge of those properties; and, perhaps most fundamentally, it conflates equilibration with reflective abstraction. Equilibration is a strictly within knowing-level phenomenon (we would argue that it is not really a process at all, but that is for another time): it might yield a 'closed structure', but it could never yield knowledge of that closure, nor of any supposedly concomitant properties of exhaustiveness or necessity. Those require the perspective of a higher knowing level. *Piaget's* discussion of necessity as a type of closure incorporated a whole system of conflations that resulted from an incomplete shift in his thinking: reflective abstraction had not replaced structural equilibration as the primary process of stage ascent.

Global and Local Necessities

There is an obvious tension in *Piaget's* account, between necessity as a property of algebraic structures and necessity as a property of knowing systems for which algebraic structures are not a sufficient basis. In fact, his process account led to a major departure from his former stuctural treatment of necessity, which had held that there was no 'true necessity' until the appearance of reversible, equilibrated concrete operational structures. He was no longer able to reduce epistemic exhaustiveness to structural exhaustiveness. In place of this structurally exhaustive *global* necessity, *Piaget* [1977b] acknowledged the existence of purely *local* necessities: 'at the preoperational level … islets of necessities are already constituted, but they are local and not tied together into stable systems' [p. 236]. The precursors for these local necessities are *signifying implications*. A signifying implication is a relationship of implication *if x then y* which is lawful; that is, there is a reason for the relationship, in terms of y being a necessary condition for x, etc. At the level of prenecessity (roughly, knowing-level 1) the reasons are implicit: 'The subject, connecting y to x in [a signifying implication, if x then y] admits generally that there must be a "reason" for this relationship, even

level 2, one needs to show in turn that it could be the result of reflective abstraction from an ability at knowing-level 1. There is an explanatory regress that runs back down the knowing levels in steps of reflective abstraction. This is analogous to the explanatory regress involved in showing what developmental sequence an ability belongs to. To establish which sequence it belongs to, one must trace back through the prerequisites of the ability to see if it has a precursor. Then one must see if the precursor has a precursor, and so on, until one arrives at the foundational precursor which marks the origin of the sequence [*Campbell and Richie*, 1983].

Understanding the Necessity of Class Inclusion

We can illustrate the differences between knowing-level and structural stage analysis by using advanced class-inclusion and seriation reasoning as examples. For instance, *Markman* [1978], *Voelin* [1976], and *Bideaud* [1980, 1981] have interpreted the emergence of a higher-order understanding of the class-inclusion principle as meaning that earlier success on the standard class-inclusion task must be due to 'empirical' rather than 'logical' solutions. *Voelin* even observed children trying out possible modifications of the class-inclusion relation, and in Chapter 5 we interpreted these as actual instances of the reflective abstraction process. *Voelin*, however, did not regard these responses as an illustration of how the necessity of class inclusion might come to be recognized. He claimed that the children's judgments of impossibility were mere 'findings of fact' that had no more logical significance than discovering that they could not lift a 30-kilogram weight [*Voelin*, 1976, p. 277]. (How could children ever acquire a logical appreciation of necessity, if such 'empirical' means are ruled out? If logical necessity were a priori and self-sufficient, it would have to built in from the start.) However, there is no evidence that children succeed on standard class-inclusion tasks by empirical methods, for instance, counting the members of the class and the subclass [*Campbell*, 1981, 1985; *Miller and Barg*, 1982]. Without much extra strain, they can solve purely verbal problems [*Wilkinson*, 1976] and problems in which the items cannot be counted [*Dagenais*, 1973; *Cormier and Dagenais*, 1983]. The interpretation of their solutions as 'empirical' is thoroughly dubious. We contend that children succeed on the class-inclusion task by 'logical' means. They make a logical inference at level 2, without explicitly appreciating its necessity. Later on, reflective abstraction of properties of this inference will make possible an explicit representation of its necessity, at level 3. The confusion about the logical necessity of class inclusion has arisen because the standard concrete operational period includes both level-2 and level-3 accomplishments, which structural accounts cannot differentiate.

The structuralist 'solution' that denigrates success on the standard class-inclusion problem as merely 'empirical' (and therefore not really concrete operational) is not the only one that has been attempted. *Cormier and Dagenais* [1983] regarded solutions to the standard class-inclusion task as genuinely logical, because children did not need to count the items and could often logically justify their answers. Because they regarded class inclusion as a genuinely logical ability, however, they were surprised to find a décalage between the ability to give logical justifications on a standard class-inclusion problem and the ability to recognize that class inclusion was logically necessary. The source of this perplexity was the structural account of concrete operations, which fails to distinguish implicit from explicit necessity. Moreover, *Cormier and Dagenais* referred to reflective abstraction (and constructive generalization) as the process by which a logical understanding of class inclusion develops. Reflective abstraction, however, is also the process by which an explicit understanding of the necessity of class inclusion could develop out of a logical understanding of class inclusion. This illustrates the incompatibility between *Piaget's* structural and process accounts of logical necessity: the process account supports a stage distinction between implicit and explicit logical necessity, whereas the structural account collapses this distinction and imposes a single structural criterion for logical necessity.

Pitfalls of Structural Task Analogies: Classes and Collections

Another structuralist response to the class-inclusion anomaly would be to grant that solutions to class-inclusion problems are genuinely logical and concrete operational. If recognizing the necessity of class inclusion belonged to a higher structural stage, it would have to be formal operational. *Markman* [1978] did in fact consider whether higher-level class-inclusion reasoning was formal operational, but rejected this possibility. She argued that there was no evidence that children actually considered alternative possibilities before drawing the conclusion that class inclusion was logically necessary. *Voelin's* [1976] observations (see Chapter 5) are prima facie counterevidence to this objection, although obviously the ability that *Markman* was examining is not 'formal operational' if one takes scientific reasoning tasks as the benchmark of formal operations. Her other reason was that an analogous task involving collections was solved by 8-year-olds, and 8-year-olds are not formal operational. Moreover, as the tasks were analogous, one could not be concrete while the other was formal. From a structural perspective, analogous tasks like these ought to be solved using the same structure, hence at the same stage. But from a knowing-level perspective, structurally analogous tasks do not have to be solved at the same knowing level.

Collections (e.g., forests, crowds, families) are groups of objects that, in *Markman's* terms, have an 'internal organization'; their members have extrinsic relations to one another that determine their membership in the collection. Classes are not internally organized in this sense; each class member individually has distinguishing characteristics necessary for class membership. An army, and the class of soldiers in that army, have the same members, but their internal organization is obviously not the same.

Suppose that collections are representable, as *Markman* has suggested, in a manner analogous to physical objects. This would imply that they are explicitly representable at level 1. The intuitive analogy between collection representations and object representations [*Markman and Seibert,* 1976; *Markman,* 1981] can be formulated more precisely. Early in knowing-level 1, children come to represent physical objects as invariants with respect to spatial transformations such as manipulation and locomotion. By mid-level 1 at the latest, children are able to represent objects whose constituents are themselves distinguishable objects, for instance, they can represent simple mechanical toys or the apparatus used in causal mechanism studies [*Bullock* et al., 1982]. Collections, whether physical aggregates or social groupings, consist of familiar kinds of things grouped according to relations that the child already understands. Hence they can be represented as a special type of object that has other objects as constituents.

Collections are a nominalistic type of representation, in that part-whole relations replace the distinct class-membership and class-inclusion relations characteristic of classes. However, traditional nominalistic approaches generally posit only one kind of part-whole relationship that will generate set-like aggregations of individuals without making a commitment to the real existence of sets or classes. Although a nominalist approach could employ many part-whole relations, this has not actually been done [*Eberle,* 1970]. Now as the same individual can belong to a heap, a crowd, a team, or a family, it is obvious that an account of collections must posit many part-whole relations. In consequence, attempts to subsume collections under standard nominalistic approaches [e.g., *Carbonnel,* 1978] fail to account for many collections with which young children are familiar.

Because collections are representable as quasi-objects, properties of collections can be implicitly represented at level 1. Part-whole comparisons can made about collections within knowing level 1. The necessity of those properties of collections can be represented at level 2. By contrast, if explicit representations of classes in extension have to be constructed by reflecting on classification procedures, they are only possible at level 2. Part-whole judgments about classes in extension (class-inclusion judgments) cannot be made until level 2. In turn, the necessity of such properties of classes can only be represented at level 3. On this analysis, the higher-level class-inclusion task requires level 3, while the supposedly analogous collection task only requires level 2. This distinction cannot be made if stages are defined in terms of structures like *Piaget's* groupings and lattices. Nor can it be made in terms of a simple structural principle like number of dimensions coordinated. Note also that the equation of explicit logical necessity with knowing-level 3 (suggested by our previous examples) does not hold across the board. It holds for the classic Piagetian logicomathematical abilities, like class-inclusion and seriation algorithms, because these belong to level 2. However, the necessity of a property of a level-1 representation, like collections, can be recognized at level 2. The necessity of a level-3 procedure could only be recognized at level 4. In general, the necessity or sufficiency of a logical inference is a *property* of that inference, and, as such, will be recognizable at the next knowing level.

Seriation at Levels 2 and 3

Let us now consider another case of level-2 and level-3 abilities that would be considered structurally similar. In this case, the abilities also develop about the same time. The ability to judge the logical sufficiency of the premises to determine a 3-term series, which belongs to knowing-level 3 (see Chapter 4), develops at the same time as another ability in the seriation domain that appears on the surface to be of comparable complexity. *Gillièron* [1977] examined children's solution strategies on two kinds of 8-term series problems. Some children were given a standard serial order problem in which they had to seriate different colored sticks, given only pairwise information about which of 2 sticks was longer. Here the physical magnitude of the sticks helped to place them in a linear order. Other children were given the task of seriating 8 colored tokens to be arranged in a vertical line, given information about which of 2 to-

tural stages, including concrete and formal operations, in terms of a task-descriptive model that yields a hierarchy of 'actions' or mathematical relations (see Chapter 4). They have presented a hypothetical sequence for the development of arithmetic operations and algebraic structures. *Commons et al.* [1982] assessed part of this sequence; otherwise, however, they have only applied the model to standard formal operational isolation of variables tasks. As we have shown, *Piaget's* structural account of formal operations is not descriptively adequate, and cannot be explanatorily adequate. *Commons and Richards'* structural account also lacks explanatory adequacy, as we showed in Chapter 4, and its ability to handle challenges to the descriptive adequacy of formal operations (in such areas as causal reasoning and the development of identity) remains to be shown. Indeed, as we showed in Chapter 4, any structural account of *any* stage will lack explanatory adequacy.

Knowing-Level 4 and Higher

In the knowing-levels hierarchy, there is a rough correspondence between postformal operations and higher knowing levels, beginning with knowing-level 4. Level 4 is reflectively abstracted from level 3, level 5 is reflectively abstracted from level 4, and so on. The character of knowing-level 4 is largely unexplored. However, at least one ability that has been analyzed as formal operational seems to be level 4. The ability to formalize deductive logical forms requires at least level 4 (see Chapter 5), because the reflective abstraction of logical form and inferential ability requires level 3 [*Moshman and Franks,* in press]. The solution of conditional reasoning problems, like the four-card problem [*Wason and Johnson-Laird,* 1972], which require an understanding of strict rules for logical implication, presupposes that relationships of implication have been decontextualized and formalized. Under this analysis, the ability to solve the four-card problem may be level 4, because there is evidence that the understanding of implication at level 3 is embedded in a network of possible causal relationships which are still being elaborated [*Markovits,* 1984]. The history of philosophy suggests that it is difficult to extract the logical relationship of implication from the complex considerations involved in evaluating theories and hypotheses; *Popper's* conception of falsification is a recent development. The ability to solve the four-card problem in its most decontextualized form is nonetheless normally analyzed as formal operational [e.g., *O'Brien and Overton,* 1980]. If our analysis of strict logical implication as level 4 is correct, it would also illustrate the point that the knowing levels are one-half cycle advanced on the corresponding Piagetian stages. In fact, a major analytic task for the knowing-levels model is to distinguish which of the standard formal operational abilities are level 4 and which are level 3.

Our knowledge of abilities that could belong to levels 5 and higher is even more rudimentary than our knowledge of level 4. Since *Commons'* systematic stage involves formalization, it may be parallel to level 4, in which case metasystematic reasoning, which involves reflection on implicit formalisms and makes use of the 'language of metalogic', would be parallel to level 5. Cross-paradigmatic reasoning, which involves formally systematizing formal systems and extracting formal properties of those systems of systems, might reach level 6. From the knowing levels standpoint, however, there is no reason to suppose that *Commons'* structural capacity descriptions, even if they are parallel to the higher knowing levels, would capture all of the potential capabilities of those knowing levels. Any such parallelism is at best partial. Furthermore, it becomes possible after knowing-level 3 to move off the simply ordered hierarchy of knowing levels and into a richer structure of developmental possibilities. We discuss this richer structure below.

Dialectical and Personality Accounts of Postformal Stages

In contrast to the conception of an unbounded stage sequence, the view that the stage structure culminates in a final postformal stage is typical of dialectical models of development [*Riegel*, 1973; *Basseches*, 1980; *Kramer*, 1983]. It is also typical of models of personality development that culminate in a final stage of mature adult personality [*Labouvie-Vief*, 1980, 1982; *Edelstein and Noam*, 1982]. The impetus for culminating stage models comes in large part from supposed deficiencies in formal thought that need to be transcended. From the dialectical standpoint, formal operations are inadequate to comprehend the true character of processes. Formal operations restrict the thinker to reasoning about closed systems rather than about open systems; and the ability to reason about open systems, dialectical processes of change, etc., requires a move beyond formal operations to dialectical operations [*Riegel*, 1973; *Basseches*, 1980]. Formal operations restrict the thinker to an inadequate world-view, which needs to be superseded by a dialectical world-view. From the standpoint of personality models, formal operations restrict the person to inadequate adolescent attitudes, such as utopianism and intolerance of other viewpoints; issues are poorly handled unless they can be resolved by strict hypothetico-deductive reasoning. To transcend these limitations, one must ascend to a postformal stage characterized by a reconciliation between the demands of formal reasoning and adequate social relationships, that is, by 'adult' personality traits [*Labouvie-Vief,* 1980, 1982; *Edelstein and Noam,* 1982].

A major weakness of these models is shared with the more orthodox structural accounts of postformal stages. The structural accounts presuppose the validity of the structural account of formal operations in order to build on it; the dialectical and personality accounts presuppose its validity in order to react against it. Given the strength of the arguments against it, the structural model of formal operations is a shaky foundation for theorizing about higher stages. In fact, an argument that some feature of formal operations must be transcended could just as easily be taken as an argument against the descriptive adequacy of formal operations.

Moreover, the dialecticians and the personality theorists tend to characterize formal operations in terms of stereotypical world-views and personality traits, which have little basis in the structural account of the stage. (*Basseches,* however, does regard postformal operations as the product of a reflection on formal operations that leads to a recognition of their limitations; he also posits formal-postformal sequences in the development of some dialectical thought schemata.) The formal model of formal operations does not deal with the epistemic assumptions necessary to describe philosophical world-views [*Kitchener and Kitchener,* 1981]. Although *Inhelder and Piaget* [1958] speculated at some length about adolescent personality, they did not tie their speculations to the formal model of formal operations, nor has anyone else. The personality theorists, in particular, have made use of *Inhelder and Piaget's* conception of a characteristically adolescent egocentrism that is overcome through accommodation to social relationships and to the world of work. *Inhelder and Piaget* never characterized adolescent egocentrism in terms of the formal model of formal operations (in fact, this cannot be done). Nor did they attempt to account for the perspective-taking process that overcomes adolescent egocentrism. In addition, the informal conception of formal operations (closest to the knowing-levels model) is not fully consistent with the stereotype of formal thought as narrow-minded and concentrated on closed systems. For every closure of previously conceived systems of possibilities to yield necessities, there is an opening onto new kinds of possibilities in thought; in fact, formal thought involves an 'explosion of possibilities' [*Piaget,* 1976]. The stereotypes of formal thought that are all too frequently employed are not adequate for specifying what postformal operations grow out of, nor, for that matter, grow beyond.

Must There Be a Culminating Stage?

An issue that has not been addressed by the proponents of a culminating postformal stage is why stage development has to terminate. In the later Piagetian model (operations to the nth degree) and in the knowing-levels model, it clearly does not have to terminate. Structural stage models that attempt to model a hierarchy of operations on operations [e.g., *Richards and Commons*, 1984] also regard the stage sequence as potentially unbounded.

Some proponents of structural stage models do, however, believe that the stage sequence has an upper bound. *Fischer's* description of stage development (see Chapter 4) terminates with level-10 principles (bidirectional mappings of bidirectional mappings of abstractions), and he contends that additional levels involving mappings between principles probably do not develop. In fact, such development would be undesirable. 'Abstractions are already so far removed from actions in the real world that further developmental levels might well be not merely useless but maladaptive' [*Fischer* et al., 1984, p. 53]. Abstractions are so distant from empirical tests at the sensory-motor level that it is easy to adopt loose and untestable conceptions, or to abuse them ideologically. *Fischer's* concerns are misplaced: error is possible at any developmental stage, but so are appropriate methods of error correction. Empirically, higher levels of mathematical reasoning (including *Commons'* examples of metasystematic and cross-paradigmatic reasoning) belong to higher knowing levels than *Fischer's* examples of level 10. Implicit in *Fischer's* objections about looseness and untestability is a philosophy of science that allows theory evaluation by empirical tests, but not by conceptual arguments; we have argued (Chapter 2) that such a philosophy of science is inadequate for developmental psychology. In fact, *Fischer* seems to have reverted to the thoroughly discredited and long-abandoned logical positivist doctrine that cognitive meaning can only derive from direct, foundational empirical content [*Suppe*, 1977]. Finally, ideological abuses frequently involve self-protective devices that prevent central assumptions of the ideology from being examined, and the way to defeat such devices is not to stay at a lower stage, but rather to ascend to the next knowing level and examine one's own assumptions [*Bickhard*, in preparation].

Kramer [1983] also objects to the infinite regress of operations on operations in the structural models, but gives no argument for wanting to avoid it. The regress is not vicious, and as a regress of potentialities, not actualities, it poses no metaphysical problems. In fact, it is strongly related to unbounded hierarchies in mathematics like the arithmetic hierarchy [*Rogers*, 1967]. To avoid the regress, *Kramer* contends, postformal thought must restructure formal thought, not just operate on it. This restructuring is not defined, however, nor is it explained how it would block the regress. A culminating postformal stage would have to be restructured so that no one could ever reflect on it, or at least so that no one would ever have a reason to reflect on it.

The demand for a culminating stage made by the personality theorists seems to derive from conflating cognitive stages with Eriksonian stages in the life cycle. The issues that adults have to face, and the corresponding adult personality ideals, have a social or cultural aspect that is not necessarily related to knowing levels. Although mature character traits may have some prerequisites in stage sequences for the development of the self (see Chapter 8) or in aspects of social development, they have little to do with higher knowing levels attained in specific domains. There may be highly neurotic individuals who have attained knowing-level 6 in some mathematical domain, and there may be mature individuals who have not gone beyond knowing-level 3 in any domain.

Insufficiency of Formal Logic for Stage Description

A valuable point made by the dialecticians [*Riegel,* 1973; *Basseches,* 1980] is that formal logic cannot be an adequate basis for a model of developmental stages. Although their critique has focused on the need to transcend formal operations, *Riegel* made the stronger argument that thought is dialectical at every stage. There have also been attempts [*Gilligan and Murphy,* 1979; *Labouvie-Vief,* 1980] to invoke *Gödel's* theorem as grounds for regarding formal logical systems as an inadequate model of a developmental stage. As *Kitchener and Kitchener* [1981] have pointed out, this argument fails to pay heed to the restrictions on the application of *Gödel's* theorem to formal deductive systems with finite methods of proof. Overlooked or not clearly stated in this debate is a more basic restriction on the relevance of formal logic to descriptive accounts of cognitive development (as we argued in Chapter 4, formal logic cannot have explanatory adequacy regardless of its descriptive adequacy). Any system of formal logic is based on the constraint of logical consistency. Consistency is a value criterion (see Chapter 8). It is a selection criterion that can be applied to the representations and procedures generated by variations and selections. Consistency is not characteristic of every aspect of thought, throughout the generation and selection of hypotheses. If it were, then inconsistency at any point would be an outright failure of the thought process. The nature of thought is to be creative and functional, and consistency is a (sometimes) functional selection criterion to apply to the creative variations involved. The dialecticians seem to have recognized this when they say that human thought is inherently dialectical. In any case, the fact that consistency is not the only fundamental criterion applicable to thought implies that formal logic cannot be an adequate basis for describing stages in the development of thought. (*Kitchener and Kitchener* [1981] approach, but do not state, this conclusion in their critique of formal operations.) The descriptive insufficiency of formal logic illustrates our general point (also made in Chapter 4) that formal functional accounts of cognition are insufficient to characterize stages, and that 'semantics' (what is known at each stage, or by each knowing level) must also be considered.

Beyond the Knowing Levels: Metareflection

So far we have presented the knowing levels in terms of each level knowing the next lower level (except the first level, which knows the environment), but without extended comment about the nature of the knowing relationship. The thesis that the nature of knowing intrinsically generates a sequence of knowing levels, which in turn generates a sequence of stages, derives from the interactive model of knowing that was presented in Chapter 3 [see also *Bickhard*, 1980a, b; *Bickhard and Richie*, 1983]. Knowing consists of interacting with the object of knowing, by differentiating it, transforming it, exploring its consequences, etc. The object that is known may be in the environment, or it may be in the next lower level of knowing. The richer structure of potential development (mentioned above) is discovered in exploring this interactive, transformational nature of knowing.

Each knowing level operates on systems at the next lower level, and either leaves them unchanged, or transforms them into new systems (or creates new systems) at that same level. There are, however, interactive knowing processes that do not fit anywhere in the hierarchy that this generates. For example, a process that would operate on systems at any level $n-1$ and generate systems at the next higher level n fits nowhere within the levels – that is, it is not explicitly differentiated at any of the levels. Reflective abstraction is a process with exactly these properties. Such a process, and its associated system, lie outside of the primary hierarchy – and serve as the base for a whole new hierarchy of potential reflective knowing, a hierarchy generated by reflecting on reflective abstraction, etc. In turn, a knowing system which can consider the relationships between these two hierarchies lies within neither of them – and will found its own hierarchy of potential reflections. The basic idea is that any relationship that generates a reflective knowing hierarchy itself lies outside that hierarchy, but founds a new one, and the relationship between the new structure and the old will initiate a recursion of the process, unboundedly.

Although the details are somewhat more complicated than in this illustration, the result is that the potentials of development can be partially described by an infinite dimensional infinite lattice, of which the knowing levels form a central, simply ordered sublattice. The implications for 'postformal' development are rather interesting. It is clear that the knowing levels proceed indefinitely, and that we have instances of knowing-level 4 and higher at least in restricted domains like mathematics. It is also clear, however, that as soon as there are sufficient instances of a hierarchy for the principle of that hierarchy to be considered – presumably three levels, for that provides two instances of the hierarchy relation – then the most interesting development will be to move out along the next available dimension – a metareflection, rather than just a reflection. From the metareflective (or infinite lattice) standpoint, indefinite development along a single simply ordered hierarchy becomes a matter of quantitative elaboration without qualitative change [e.g., *Kramer*, 1983], while the principle of unbounded development [e.g., *Commons* et al., 1982] is rediscovered in the unboundedness of the dimensions.

The formal treatment of the structure of developmental potentialities intrinsic to the ontology of the interactive knowing model quickly becomes enormously rich in mathematical structure. Assume first of all that knowing systems can be modeled by Turing machines (there are strong reasons to believe that Turing machines are not sufficiently powerful [*Bickhard and Richie*, 1983, footnote 23], but this discussion will accept Turing machines as a first approximation). Now shift to a level of consideration in which everything has been replaced by its Gödel number. The universe is now constituted by the natural numbers N. Consider this to be level zero. Some of those numbers will be Gödel numbers of Turing machines: denominate the class of Turing machine numbers as level 1. Some Turing machines, in turn, will operate only on other Turing machines: call that class level 2, and so on. This structure is homomorphic to the simple knowing-levels hierarchy.

In this simply ordered hierarchy, each Turing machine is considered to operate on elements of a particular class and to generate via those operations resultant elements of the same class. But this assumption need not necessarily hold: a Turing machine, considered as a realization of a transformation, need not have its domain and codomain (range) equal to each other. Begin as above with class zero of all Gödel numbers, but now categorize Turing machines in terms of the ordered pairs of their domain class number and their codomain class number. Each Turing machine, thus, would be classified by an ordered pair $\langle i, j \rangle$ where i is the number of its domain and j is the number of its codomain. Such single classifying natural numbers will always exist for any such domain and codomain because the ordered pairs themselves can be bijectively mapped onto the natural numbers, B: $N \times N \to N$. Beginning with class zero, then, the first class to be differentiated by this procedure will the class of Turing machines whose domain and codomain are class zero; this class of Turing machines will have the index number of B($\langle 0, 0 \rangle$). The procedure will now generate the classes of Turing machines with domain 0 and codomain B($\langle 0, 0 \rangle$), with domain B($\langle 0, 0 \rangle$) and codomain 0, and with domain B($\langle 0, 0 \rangle$) and codomain B($\langle 0, 0 \rangle$) – these will have the index numbers of B($\langle 0, B(\langle 0, 0 \rangle) \rangle$), B($\langle B(\langle 0, 0 \rangle), 0 \rangle$), and B($\langle B(\langle 0, 0 \rangle), B(\langle 0, 0 \rangle) \rangle$) respectively. Recursive application of the procedure generates the full infinite lattice corresponding to the bijection B: $N \times N \to N$.

Even this does not exhaust the structure of potentialities, however. Consider a Turing machine whose arguments and resultants have index numbers with a functional relationship, such as $\langle i, f(i) \rangle$ for some function f. Within the lattice defined in the above paragraph, such a Turing machine would be classified with the superset of all possible i's as its domain, and with the superset of all possible f(i)'s as its codomain. Such a Turing machine would be included in the above lattice, but its special properties would not be differentiated. One possible approach to capturing this additional structure would be to construe all argument and resultant index pairs as being in the form $\langle i, f(i) \rangle$, to replace i and f(i) with the Gödel numbers for $\{i\}$ and f, and to then apply the bijection B. When f is a constant function, $f(i) \equiv j$, then we would have the cases explicitly treated in the previous paragraph, but when f is not a constant function a still richer structure would obtain. Only at this level of structure do we begin to formally capture the crudely defined lattice discussed earlier which is generated by the process of reflective abstraction, the metareflective lattice: reflective abstraction considered in terms of its argument and resultant relationships would be characterized by $\langle i, B(\langle i,i \rangle) \rangle$, i.e., f for reflective abstraction is *not* a constant function, but instead $f(i) = B(\langle i,i \rangle)$. It is not at all clear that even this would fully characterize the structure of the potentialities. The full structure would appear to have deep relationships with other not fully characterized structures within the theory of effective computability [*Rogers*, 1967].

8. Development of the Self and of Values

Development of the Self and Identity

We have contended that the levels of knowing are neither structure nor content specific, and, thus, that they generalize to all areas of development. So far we have only treated standard cognitive developmental domains. To illustrate this point about generality, we will present a schematic outline of a knowing-level model of identity development. The presentation will be an outline because of space limitations; it will be schematic because of the state of the art in this area. The critical conceptions that must be dealt with are those of 'self' and 'identity', and there are no clear or consensual versions of those. Our approach will be to present schematic *explications* of these concepts in terms of the levels of knowing, from which the general developmental implications follow readily.

A strictly level-1 child can think only in interaction with the environment: truly internal interactions require a second level. Within this first level, the child will develop meaningful ('meaningful' requires its own explication) heuristics and goals for dealing with the material and social environments (and will differentiate those environments from each other), including, in particular, those primary others of the immediate family. In terms of these ways of dealing with the world, the child will *be* a person, will *have* a *self*, but will not *know* that self. Selfhood is implicit in the child's ways of being in the world, but cannot become explicit without the second knowing level.

With the advent of level 2, the child can come to know his or her own self from within that second level. This knowing may involve explicit sentences held as beliefs – the classic self-conception – but more fundamentally consists of metastrategies for managing the child's being in diverse kinds of life situations. Examples would include heuristics for successfully creating (or 'successfully' avoiding) play situations with other children. Such metastrategies may implicitly presuppose various good and bad things to be true of the child, but will not in general explicitly believe them. The child already has an identity (a set of ways, perhaps implicit, of being in the world), but cannot know or consider or revise that identity yet.

The child at the first level, then, implicitly has a self, but cannot know that self. At the second level, the child knows that self, and thereby has an implicit representation of his or her self. At the third level, the child can know that self-representation, thereby making it explicit. Now the child can compare his or her self to a system of alternatives, judge it against values, and construct it in accordance with those judgments. This examination and construction of the self, in terms of the aspects of life which require a self-definition, *is* the process of identity formation. It will be problematic or a crisis according to the kinds and severities of difficulties that are encountered. Identity *is* the situatedness of the self with respect to (aspects of) life.

In a general schematic way, then, the issues of self and identity formation are addressed quite naturally by the levels of knowing model, without any contortions to accommodate aporetic structures or contents.

Blasi and Hoeffel [1974] argue that it is not possible to account for the development of the self in terms of reflective abstraction [see also *Broughton*, 1981b]. In part, their objections are based on the restriction of formal operations to scientific reasoning about physical situations, a limitation that does not apply to the knowing-levels approach (see Chapter 4). However, they also object to reflective abstraction as a basis for self-awareness. They do not believe that self-awareness could arise from internal reflection on knowing acts; instead, self-awareness or reflectivity must be built in to the process of knowing from the start. 'There is no knowing ... without a transparent presence to the self, that is, without an awareness of the act of knowing, which is simultaneous with and intrinsic to the act itself' [*Blasi and Hoeffel*, 1974, p. 357]. We see no reason for this requirement: lower animals provide many examples of knowing that is not reflective. Furthermore, such a position must explain how 'intrinsically reflective knowing' could emerge, phylogenetically and ontogenetically. If reflective knowing about knowing does not emerge from a logically and temporally prior knowing, then how could it emerge [*Bickhard*, 1979]? As developmentalists, we are committed to explaining how various properties of knowing emerge, rather than taking them for granted, or positing their origin out of nothing; moreover, the foundation for the knowing-levels model [*Bickhard*, 1980a] does include a model of the evolution of reflective knowing, and an account of its emergence in the individual (see Chapters 3 and 5). *Blasi and Hoeffel* [1974] seem to be aware that there is no scientific basis for their claim, because they conclude that 'the domain of subjectivity ... is impenetrable *as such* to the methods of scientific experimentation' [p. 361].

The Development of Values

Our schematic outline of the development of the self and identity illustrates the potential generality of the knowing-levels approach; such an approach is not intrinsically limited to classical cognitive issues. In this section, we will present a similarly schematic explication of the development of values. Values are a crucial and mostly neglected aspect of development. Their explication involves some distinctions of fundamental importance in psychology and development, distinctions that can only be made in terms of epistemic reflection. The knowing-levels approach is not just capable of explicating values and their development; it is necessary for explicating them.

Our discussion presents an explication of values, then explores a few consequences of that explication. Preparatory to the explication of values, we distinguish, within the underlying interactive model, between instrumental and satisfaction relationships in a goal-directed system. We then apply these distinctions to the levels-of-knowing hierarchy, resulting in a particular kind of relationship that we propose as an explication of values. Specifically, we analyze values as goals that have other, lower-level goals as satisfiers – as goals that are about other goals. In discussing the consequences of the proposed explication of values, we focus primarily on the *role* of values in development. We also explicate a particular *kind* of value that is of central importance, both synchronically and diachronically, but is even more difficult to understand from standard perspectives than are most values.

Instrumental Relationships

Explicating value requires us to distinguish two kinds of relationships that pertain to goal-directed systems. The distinction must be made between an *instrumental* relationship and what might be called a *satisfaction* relationship. An instrumental relationship is the standard means-end relationship in any goal-directed system. The satisfaction relationship must be differentiated from this more common conception. We begin with a preliminary analysis of the instrumental relationship, then consider satisfaction.

If a goal-directed system calls on a subsystem as part of its interactive strategy for accomplishing the higher system's goal, that calling-relationship constitutes the overall system's knowledge of the potential instrumental relationship between the two subsystems. The actual interactions of the subsystem in a particular case may or may not succeed in maintaining or transforming the environment in some way that serves as a precondition for further interactions which result in the relevant environmental goal conditions. If the lower system is actually useful for accomplishing the higher system's goal, then those subsystem interactions will in fact be instrumental for the higher system's goal. In general, a goal-directed system's call to a subsystem constitutes an implicit 'expectation' that that lower system's interactions will in fact be instrumental for the current goal. There are some subtleties involved in instrumental relationships. It is necessary to distinguish relations of the higher system to the subsystem, the subsystem's interactions, and the environmental concomitants of those interactions, because these are 'instrumental' in slightly different senses. Nonetheless, the basic intuition of an instrumental relationship is highly familiar, especially in this information-processing cybernetic age.

Satisfaction Relationships

There is another kind of relationship in goal-directed systems that is less often emphasized. The relationship between the goal representation in the higher system and the environmental goal conditions that correspond to it (when it has been achieved) is just as critical as the instrumental relationship to understanding the overall system, but it is not itself instrumental. The goal conditions *satisfy* the goal representations; they *instantiate* what the goal representations represent. There is no instrumental 'for the sake of' relationship here, but rather a direct, perhaps consummatory, satisfaction of the goal.

There are varieties of this satisfaction relationship. Two that we will consider for illustration are 'expressive' and 'detection' relationships. In some cases, what is important is that the goal conditions depend for their existence on the creative agency of the system; creating the goal conditions is a relatively free activity of the agent – relatively unconstrained by the environment. Examples might include a dance performance, or the creation of a literary work. In such cases those goal conditions (which may themselves be activities, or the direct products of activities) not only satisfy the goal representations, but can be said to *express* those goal representations. Another version of this noninstrumental satisfaction relationship can be found if we consider that the subsystem that is called on by the higher system may not create or transform anything at all, but rather may detect, or fail to detect, something, and that

Unfolding

Developmentally, an important relationship among values is the dual of the satisfaction relationship: the relationship not from a value to the lower-level system (property) that satisfies it, but rather the relationship from an underlying organization to a new value that develops above it using that organization as its paradigm satisfier. A higher-level value that develops with a lower-level value (or interactive organization) as its satisfier constitutes a selection, a construction, within the realm of all the possible higher values which the given lower system would satisfy. Such a higher-level value is an explication, an unfolding, of a value that is *implicit* in the lower-level system. It refines and deepens the values already implicit in the person and in his or her life.

Of course, the explicated unfolding of one value already implicit in the person will not be assured of being consonant with other values, both implicit and explicit, in the person, and may lead to attempts to change both lower values and lower functional organizations. Value development can yield autonomous internal change. Any further development, in fact, is subject to the potential issue of whether or not it satisfies relevant higher-level goals about the given level of interaction, is subject to the potential issue of whether or not it satisfies relevant values. Value development leads and constrains all other development.

Our conception of values as the leading edge of development has a number of implications for developmental psychology, which we can only state here without significant elaboration. The importance of values in our account of development indicates a convergence between the concerns of the interactive model and those of *action theory*. In a general sense, the interactive model and the knowing-levels model are a type of action theory. The focus of action theory is on intentional action and its development [e.g., *Eckensberger and Meacham*, 1984]. We might add that an explanation of intentional action requires a model of consciousness and of knowing-level relationships, and the information-processing conceptions favored by some advocates of action theory [e.g., *Chapman and Skinner*, 1984] will therefore not be adequate for this task.

Another consequence of our analysis is a fundamental similarity between epistemological and moral norms; both kinds of norms must be understood as selection criteria used by a goal-directed organism whose goals evolve through the developmental unfolding process. The similarity between epistemological and moral norms has been emphasized by a few philosophers belonging to widely differing schools [*Wittgenstein*, 1958; *Peirce* – scc

Bernstein, 1971, and *Potter,* 1967; *Heidegger,* 1962; *Kelley,* in press; *Boyl* al., 1976]. This similarity is not usually recognized because of the prevai̇ᴜᴜ fact-value or is-ought dichotomies. Thus, in Chapter 7, we analyzed logical consistency as a value criterion for thought (and not the only or the highest value criterion).

Finally, our view that values emerge in development as unfoldings of the self is compatible with the eudaimonistic conception of a morality of self-actualization [e.g., *Norton,* 1976; *Veatch,* 1980]. It is opposed to externally derived and imposed concepts of duty, such as those of *Kant* [1785], *Rawls* [1971], and *Habermas* [1979]. Prevailing approaches to moral development [e.g., *Kohlberg,* 1971; *Colby* et al., 1983; *Turiel and Davidson,* 1985] accept a morality of duty and strive to isolate moral development from the development of values in general, and of the self. These approaches are untenable. Moral development is bound up with, and cannot be divorced from, the development of the self [see also *Campbell,* 1984].

Self-Referential Values

Some values have a distinct and important relationship to the functioning and ontology of the person, and therefore to development. We have discussed how higher level values may induce changes in lower level organization. Such changes are of major importance in development, but they require that a distinction be possible between the value that is inducing the change and the organization that is being changed, and that distinction is not always possible. Some values make implicit reference to, have as potential satisfiers, are about the entire person, including all extant levels of knowing, and including themselves. Such self-referential values are about the whole person, but they intrinsically do not and cannot have instrumental access to the whole person. To have instrumental access to the whole person, they would have to be outside the person and a part of that person at the same time. Self-referential values intrinsically *cannot* be instrumentally instantiated or satisfied. Examples would include the values of being caring, of being spontaneous, of being at peace with oneself in the world. One cannot deliberately, instrumentally, be caring, or at peace in the world. Not all self-referential values are so 'existential': enjoying jazz is also an instance of a self-referential value. All self-referential values, when attained, are experienced more as realizations than accomplishments – from enjoying jazz to existential authenticity (authenticity is the expression, in the technical sense given above, of a particular self-referential value).

Attempts to approach self-referential values as instrumental goals can be very confusing and disorganizing, even destructive to the person: such attempts can distort and disrupt the autonomous activity of experiencing. They are implicit attempts to make oneself an instrumental object, and that denies and potentially does damage to central aspects of one's ontology. Noninstrumental understandings of such values, and of the noninstrumental principles involved in them, are important, difficult, and not common. The noninstrumental instantiation of such values in one's person and life constitutes some of the farther reaches of human potentiality [*Bickhard*, in preparation].

Our analysis of self-referential values contradicts, or at least limits, instrumental, problem-oriented approaches to psychotherapy: one cannot set out to be more self-actualizing or more authentic today. Insofar as self-referential values (like autonomy or being caring) are concerned, problem-oriented approaches to child-rearing and socialization are also inappropriate.

Implications of Our Analysis of Values: Hermeneutics

These explications clearly entail that values are ontologically and developmentally central to the person, to the self, and to identity. Analogous points apply to the dimensions of the developmental lattice as well as to the levels of knowing. We will not explore these issues further here; they are on the frontiers of the interactive approach, and we lack space to pursue them. Also for another time is the relationship between affect and values: an interactive model of emotions was mentioned in Chapter 3, but its elaboration is a major task in its own right.

Similarly, we will not explore the social ontological constitution of values, the self, and identity: to do so, we would have to explicate the emergence of the social level of ontology out of the ontology of agents and actions. Even without an explication of the social basis for values, however, our presentation of the interactive model suffices to indicate some fundamental convergences and divergences with another approach to the social-linguistic ontology of human beings – that of *hermeneutics*. The interactive model explains the emergence of social realities, called situation conventions, out of the relationships among the representations held by agents. It explicates language as a system of conventionalized operations on situation conventions [*Bickhard*, 1980b]. A consequence of these explications is that situation conventions consist in large part of potentialities for further conversation or linguistic interaction [*Bickhard*, in press] – much of social reality is linguistic. Moreover, much of the ontology of the person, self, or personality is constituted in terms of the manner of constructive participation in situation conventions; in terms of social self-presentation, negotiation, and construction in situation conventions; and in terms of longer-run social realities, ranging from institutional roles to group memberships to intimate relationships, in which the individual constitutively participates and is thereby constituted. The ontology of the person is massively social, and because the social is largely linguistic, the person is thereby massively constituted in terms of language. In terms of the levels of knowing, and in terms of comparable hierarchies in the ontology and epistemology of situation conventions [*Bickhard*, 1980b], this social ontology of the person partakes deeply of reflectively layered interpretations of one's self and life and values regarding these things [*Taylor*, 1977]. In all of these ways, the interactive model is highly convergent with hermeneutics. In addition, the central properties of language stressed in hermeneutic accounts – the hermeneutic circle, and the historicity of language – turn out to be consequences of the interactive model of language.

We have only sketched the convergences with hermeneutics – the social and language models would have to be considerably elaborated to explore them further. The divergences, however, can be presented a little more explicitly. Most centrally, the interactive model grounds the social and linguistic ontologies of the person in presocial and prelinguistic ontologies: level-1 knowing, the macroevolutionary sequence of knowing, learning, emotions, and consciousness, and the intrinsic constraints that emerge from them. Prelinguistic development in infancy, for instance, is a crucial basis for, and source of constraints on, the individual's later development. With development, all aspects of the person partake more and more of the constitutive participation in and reciprocal constitution by social and language ontologies, but the presocial, prelinguistic ground and its constraints are never lost, and can never be fully transcended. In this respect the interactive model diverges sharply from those themes in hermeneutics that subsume the ontology of the person within the social-linguistic community, reducing the person to a local nexus of social relationships [*Wittgenstein*, 1958; *Heidegger*, 1962; *Ricoeur*, 1970; *Gadamer*, 1975; *Habermas*, 1979; see also *Howard*, 1982; *Harré*, 1984; *Spence*, 1982; *Eagle*, 1984]. From the interactive perspective, such a position recognizes that the transcendental conditions for one's being in the world (i.e., the conditions necessary for the possibility of humanly being in the world) are largely constituted in one's social-historical-linguistic situation. It utterly fails to recognize or explicate the transcendental conditions for the individual's constitutive participation in such historical-social-linguistic situations. Knowing, learning, emotions, and consciousness, and their intrinsic constraints and potentialities, are necessary for social, historical, and linguistic realities to exist, and for the individual to constitutively participate in them.

Moreover, these grounding human ontologies and their constraints have consequences for the hermeneutic nature of human existence. They constrain the possibilities of the hermeneutic construction of the person. They not only limit what could be constructed at all, but also limit what could be constructed that would be consonant with the grounding ontology. Constructions of the person may, in fact, be in error with respect to the underlying human nature on which such constructions are grounded. The possibility of intrinsic error in the construction of the person, for example, in the unfolding of one's values, is introduced. The grounding constraints that derive from human psychology introduce transcendent criteria for the ontologies of persons, including ethics and values, that potentially eliminates the arbitrariness and relativity of an ungrounded strictly hermeneutic conception of human existence [*Rorty*, 1982]. It must be noted, however, that such an existence claim for ethical and value criteria does not provide an automatic or immutably certain epistemology for those criteria. Ethics and values that are consonant with fundamental human nature will be dependent in many ways on the particulars of one's social-historical situation [*MacIntyre*, 1981]. Moreover, the intrinsic grounding criteria for such consonance can only be approached in the same partial and tentative epistemology as any other aspect of reality. Thus, interactivism yields neither a false objectivism and certainty about values, nor a hollow relativism [*Bernstein*, 1983]. Such points must receive a more adequate development elsewhere.

Our explication of value development has been concerned most of all with the essential role that epistemic reflection plays in the ontology of values. If this is a valid approach to values and their development, then a developmental model that lacks epistemic reflection and levels of knowing cannot possibly explicate the nature of values or their role in development.

9. Conclusion

We have shown (in Chapter 5) how the knowing-levels approach to developmental stages provides an explication of the crucial developmental process of reflective abstraction. We have also shown how our approach solves a number of problems, such as the development of logical necessity (Chapter 6), 'postformal' development (Chapter 7), and the development of self, identity, and values (Chapter 8), all of which are poorly handled by the structural approach. When combined with the critique of structural stage models that was presented in Chapter 4, these arguments, we believe, make a strong case for the knowing-levels model.

Much current theorizing about development obviously indicates dissatisfaction with the limitations of the prevailing structural accounts. Some of it, including *Piaget's* last work, also indicates an increased interest in constructive developmental processes, such as reflective abstraction. The knowing-levels approach develops and extends both of these themes in recent thought about development.

A case in point is the increasing recognition of the inadequacy of one of *Piaget's* structural stages, formal operations (see Chapter 4). Over the last 15 years, a good deal of research and theory have converged on the knowing-levels alternative to formal operations, knowing-level 3. Various attempts have been made to characterize advanced reasoning in terms of acceptance of lack of closure [*Lunzer,* 1978]; a modal logic of necessity and possibility [*Piéraut-LeBonniec,* 1980]; and a transition from implicit to explicit logical necessity [*Moshman and Timmons,* 1982]. None of these approaches, however, went so far as to challenge *Piaget's* stage boundaries for formal operations, or to reject structural models of stages and stage properties. None took the final step of redefining stages in terms of levels of knowing, in terms directly relevant to developmental processes.

Another case in point is the current debate about the very existence of reflective abstraction or reflective knowing as a developmental process (see Chapter 4 and 5). There is a deep division between those approaches to development [e.g., *Piaget,* 1977a; *Kuhn,* 1983] that regard reflective abstraction as a genuine developmental process and an object of research interest, and those that do not acknowledge it [e.g., *Pascual-Leone*, 1980; *Fischer*, 1980; *Commons and Richards*, 1984a] or seek to replace it with vaguely defined and insufficiently powerful processes [e.g., *Gelman*, 1982; *Brown*, 1982].

Any evaluation of the knowing-levels approach must recognize that it is highly programmatic. Much work still needs to be done in producing detailed models of representation and reasoning processes within the approach. Indeed, the knowing-levels approach calls for detailed analyses of representation in each psychological domain (not task domain) in which development is to be explained. The domain problem pervades the study of cognitive and social development [*Richie*, 1984]. It will not do to use descriptive structural analyses of sets of tasks to define domains or to characterize representation (see Chapter 4). Moreover, the strongly 'vertical' or sequential character of the knowing-levels model, and the focus on prerequisites and precursors of current abilities, requires special attention to the foundations of representation in infant perception and action systems [*Campbell and Richie*, 1983].

Considerable theoretical development is still required to produce full-fledged empirical research programs within the knowing-levels approach. The fact that the approach is programmatic does not prevent it from being rationally evaluated, however. Like any programmatic proposal, it can be challenged by conceptual arguments. Any approach to development, no matter how much empirical research has made use of it, must be evaluated in conceptual terms as well as empirical terms: although the Piagetian structuralist approach and the information-processing approach have both generated large amounts of empirical research, their merits cannot be determined on empirical grounds alone. Thus we have identified some empirical problems (e.g., the necessity of class inclusion) which are anomalous (not readily soluble) for the structural approach, but are readily soluble for the knowing-levels approach. We have also pointed to conceptual problems in the structural approach (e.g., the fact that structural accounts are only descriptions of task accomplishments) that are solved by the knowing-levels approach. These arguments indicate that the knowing-levels approach is promising enough to merit further development and testing.

Such considerations need mentioning, because of the conceptions of science that still prevail in psychology (see Chapter 2). Although contemporary philosophy of science [e.g., *Suppe*, 1977; *Laudan*, 1977] recognizes the importance of conceptual arguments in evaluating theories, the views of science most prevalent among psychologists do not. Too many psychologists still subscribe to logical positivism, which has no place for conceptual considerations at all [*Bickhard* et al., 1985], or to Lakatosian philosophy of science (see Chapter 2) which restricts theory evaluation to the progress of empirical research programs, and regards conceptual considerations as objects of faith or commitment, not to be evaluated by critical arguments.

Underlying our case for the knowing-levels approach is a conception of the basic problems in developmental psychology that any adequate theory ought to be able to solve. We have contended that developmental psychology needs an explanatory account of psychological processes, and of the developmental metaprocesses that change psychological processes. The centrality of developmental processes, and the subordination of stages to processes, are part of this conception of what developmental psychology is all about. Whether the knowing-levels approach ultimately proves adequate to solve these problems, they are problems that have not been addressed by most developmental theorizing to date, and that need to be taken seriously by future theories.

The knowing-levels approach provides an important alternative for developmental psychologists who must evaluate *Piaget's* legacy and decide how to move beyond it. In Chapter 1, we argued that there were distinct themes in *Piaget's* approaches to his foundational epistemological concerns: structuralism, functionalism, and an incompletely developed interactivism and consequent constructivism. Currently, *Piaget* is understood in terms of his structuralism, or, somewhat less often, his functionalism; rarely are *Piaget's* interactivist and constructivist perspectives given priority [see *von Glasersfeld*, 1981, 1984, who emphasizes *Piaget's* constructivism, but with little emphasis on the underlying interactivism]. Conservative Piagetians [e.g., *Voelin*, 1976; *Neimark*, 1979; *Overton and Newman*, 1982] – those who prefer his theory as it was before 1965 – have retained the structuralist approach and deemphasized both functionalism and *Piaget's* concerns about interaction and epistemic reflection. The standard alternative is to replace *Piaget's* structural models with functional, information-processing models. This approach is constantly recommended by non-Piagetians [e.g., *Boden*, 1979; *Sternberg and Powell*, 1983] and is now being adopted by some Piagetians as well [e.g., *Blanchet*, 1980; *Karmiloff-Smith*, 1985]. Structuralist and functionalist approaches can also be combined, as they are in the best-known neo-Piagetian stage models [*Pascual-Leone*, 1980; *Fischer*, 1980; *Case*, 1978]. We have argued, however, that neither structuralist nor functionalist ontologies are capable in principle of solving the epistemological problems

Bideaud, J.: Les expériences d'apprentissage de l'inclusion et la théorie opératoire. Psychol. fr. 26: 238–258 (1981).

Blanchet, A.: Etude génétique des significations et des modèles utilisés par l'enfant lors des solutions de problèmes (Imprimerie Nationale, Genève 1980).

Blanshard, B.: Reason and analysis (Open Court, LaSalle 1962).

Blasi, A.; Hoeffel, E.C.: Adolescence and formal operations. Hum. Dev. 17: 344–363 (1974).

Block, N.: Introduction: What is functionalism? In Block, Readings in philosophy and psychology, vol. 1 (Harvard University Press, Cambridge 1980a).

Block, N.: Troubles with functionalism; in Block, Readings in philosophy and psychology, vol. 1 (Harvard, Cambridge 1980b).

Bochenski, I.M.: A history of formal logic (Chelsea Publishing Co., New York 1970).

Boden, M.A.: Piaget (Fontana, Glasgow 1979).

Bohm, D.: Causality and chance in modern physics (Routledge & Kegan Paul, London 1957).

Boyle, J.; Grisez, G.; Tollefsen, O.: Free choice: a self-referential argument (Notre Dame University Press, Notre Dame 1976).

Braine, M.D.S.; Rumain, B.: Logical reasoning; in Flavell, Markman, Handbook of child psychology, vol. 3: Cognitive development (Wiley, New York 1983).

Brainerd, C.J.: The stage question in cognitive-development theory. Behav. Brain Sci. 1: 173–213 (1978).

Broughton, J.M.: Piaget's structural developmental psychology. II. Logic and psychology. Hum. Dev. 24: 195–224 (1981a).

Broughton, J.M.: Piaget's structural developmental psychology. IV. Knowledge without a self and without history. Hum. Dev. 24: 320–346 (1981b).

Brown, A.L.: Learning and development: the problems of compatibility, access, and induction. Hum. Dev. 25: 89–115 (1982).

Brown, A.L.; Bransford, J.D.; Ferrara, R.A.; Campione, J.C.: Learning, remembering, and understanding; in Flavell, Markman, Handbook of child psychology, vol. 3: Cognitive development (Wiley, New York 1983).

Buchdahl, G.: Metaphysics and the philosophy of science (MIT Press, Cambridge 1969).

Bullock, M.: Causal reasoning and developmental change over the preschool years. Hum. Dev. 28: 169–191 (1985).

Bullock, M.; Gelman, R.; Baillargeon, R.: The development of causal reasoning; in Friedman, The developmental psychology of time (Academic Press, New York 1982).

Bynum, T.W.; Thomas, J.A.; Weitz, L.J.: Truth-functional logic in formal operational thinking: Inhelder and Piaget's evidence. Devl Psychol. 7: 129–132 (1972).

Campbell, D.T.: Evolutionary epistemology; in Schilpp, The philosophy of Karl Popper (Open Court, LaSalle 1974).

Campbell, R.L.: Linguistic difficulties in the class-inclusion task (University of Texas, Austin, unpubl. 1981).

Campbell, R.L.: Moral development theory: a critique of its Kantian presuppositions (University of Texas, Austin, unpubl. 1984).

Campbell, R.L.: Class-inclusion: logical and mathematical prerequisites (University of Texas, Austin, unpubl. 1985).

Campbell, R.L.; Bickhard, M.H.: A deconstruction of Fodor's anticonstructivism (Jean Piaget Society, Philadelphia, unpubl. 1985).

Campbell, R.L.; Richie, D.M.: Problems in the theory of developmental sequences: prerequisites and precursors. Hum. Dev. 26: 156–172 (1983).

Carbonnel, S.: Classes collectives et classes logiques dans la pensée naturelle. Archs Psychol. *46:* 1–20 (1978).

Case, R.: Intellectual development from birth to adulthood: a neo-Piagetian interpretation; in Siegler, Children's thinking: what develops? (Erlbaum, Hillsdale 1978).

Cavanaugh, J.C.; Perlmutter, M.: Metamemory: a critical examination. Child Dev. *53:* 11–28 (1982).

Chapman, M.; Skinner, E.A.: Action in development/development in action; in Frese, Sabini, Goal-directed behavior: psychological theory and research on action (Erlbaum, Hillsdale 1984).

Chomsky, N.: Review of Skinner's 'Verbal behavior'. Language *35:* 26–58 (1959).

Chomsky, N.: Aspects of the theory of syntax (MIT Press, Cambridge 1965).

Chomsky, N.: Reflections on language (Pantheon, New York 1975).

Colby, A.; Kohlberg, L.; Gibbs, J.; Lieberman, M.: A longitudinal study of moral judgment. Monogr. Soc. Res. Child Dev. *48:* 1–2, ser. No. 200 (1983).

Commons, M.L.; Richards, F.A.: A general model of stage theory; in Commons, Richards, Armon, Beyond formal operations: late adolescent and adult cognitive development (Praeger, New York 1984a).

Commons, M.L.; Richards, F.A.: Applying the general stage model; in Commons, Richards, Armon, Beyond formal operations: late adolescent and adult cognitive development (Praeger, New York 1984b).

Commons, M.L.; Richards, F.A.; Kuhn, D.: Systematic and metasystematic reasoning: a case for levels of reasoning beyond Piaget's stage of formal operations. Child Dev. *53:* 1058–1069 (1982).

Cooper, R.G., Jr.: Early number development: discovering number space with addition and subtraction; in Sophian, Origins of cognitive skills (Erlbaum, Hillsdale 1984).

Cormier, P.; Dagenais, Y.: Class-inclusion developmental levels and logical necessity. Int. J. Behav. Dev. *6:* 1–14 (1983).

Cunningham, M.: Intelligence: its organization and development (Academic Press, New York 1972).

Dagenais, Y.: Analyse de la cohérence entre les groupements d'addition des classes, de multiplication des classes et d'addition des relations asymétriques (Université de Montréal, Montréal, unpubl. 1973).

Dennett, D.: Brainstorms (Bradford, Montgomery 1978).

Eagle, M.: Recent developments in psychoanalysis (McGraw-Hill, New York 1984).

Eberle, R.A.: Nominalistic systems (Reidel, Dordrecht 1970).

Eckensberger, L.H.; Meacham, J.A.: The essentials of action theory: a framework for discussion. Hum. Dev. *27:* 166–172 (1984).

Edelstein, W.; Noam, G.: Regulatory structures of the self and 'postformal' stages in adulthood. Hum. Dev. *25:* 407–422 (1982).

Ennis, R.H.: Conceptualization of children's logical competence: Piaget's propositional logic and an alternative proposal; in Siegel, Brainerd, Alternatives to Piaget: critical essays on the theory (Academic Press, New York 1978).

Field, H.: Mental representation; in Block, Readings in philosophy and psychology, vol. 2 (Harvard, Cambridge 1981).

Fischer, K.W.: A theory of cognitive development: the control and construction of hierarchies of skills. Psychol. Rev. *87:* 477–531 (1980).

Fischer, K.W.; Hand, H.H.; Russell, S.: The development of abstractions in adolescence and adulthood; in Commons, Richards, Armon, Beyond formal operations: late adolescent and adult cognitive development (Praeger, New York 1984).

Flavell, J.H.: Cognitive development (Prentice-Hall, Englewood Cliffs 1977).

Flavell, J.H.: Structures, stages and sequences in cognitive development; in Collins, The concept of development (Erlbaum, Hillsdale 1982).

Flavell, J.H.; Wellman, H.M.: Metamemory; in Kail, Hagen, Perspectives on the development of memory and cognition (Erlbaum, Hillsdale 1977).

Flavell, J.H.; Wohlwill, J.F.: Formal and functional aspects of cognitive development; in Elkind, Flavell, Cognitive development: essays in honor of Jean Piaget (Oxford University Press, New York 1969).

Fodor, J.: Some reflections on L.S. Vygotsky's 'Thought and language'. Cognition 1: 83–95 (1972).

Fodor, J.: Methodological solipsism considered as a research strategy in cognitive psychology; in Haugeland, Mind design (MIT, Cambridge 1981).

Fodor, J.: The modularity of mind: an essay on faculty psychology (MIT, Cambridge 1983).

Fodor, J.; Pylyshyn, Z.: How direct is visual perception? Some reflections on Gibson's ecological approach. Cognition 9: 139–196 (1981).

Gadamer, H.-G.: Truth and method (Continuum, New York 1975).

Gardner, H.: The quest for mind (Knopf, New York 1973).

Gelman, R.: Accessing one-to-one correspondence: still another paper on conservation. Br. J. Psychol. 73: 209–220 (1982).

Gelman, R.; Baillargeon, R.: A review of some Piagetian concepts; in Flavell, Markman, Handbook of child psychology, vol. 3: Cognitive development (Wiley, New York 1983).

Gibbs, J.C.: Kohlberg's moral stage theory: a Piagetian revision. Hum. Dev. 22: 89–112 (1979).

Gillièron, C.: Serial order and vicariant order: the limits of isomorphism. Archs Psychol. 45: 183–204 (1977).

Gilligan, C.; Murphy, J.M.: Development from adolescence to adulthood: the philosopher and the dilemma of the fact; in Kuhn, Intellectual development beyond childhood (Jossey-Bass, San Francisco 1979).

Glasersfeld, E. von: The concepts of adaptation and viability in a radical constructivist theory of knowledge; in Sigel, Brodzinsky, Golinkoff, New directions in Piagetian theory and practice (Erlbaum, Hillsdale 1981).

Glasersfeld, E. von: An introduction to radical constructivism; in Watzlawick, The invented reality (Norton, New York 1984).

Greeno, J.G.; Riley, M.S.; Gelman, R.: Conceptual competence and children's counting. Cognitive Psychol. 16: 94–143 (1984).

Habermas, J.: Moral development and ego identity; in Habermas, Communication and the evolution of society (Beacon, Boston 1979).

Hakes, D.T.: The development of metalinguistic abilities: what develops? In Kuczaj, Language development: language, thought, and culture (Erlbaum, Hillsdale 1982).

Harré, R.: The principles of scientific thinking (University of Chicago Press, Chicago 1970).

Harré, R.: Personal being (Harvard University Press, Cambridge 1984).

Harré, R.; Madden, E.H.: Causal powers (Blackwell, Oxford 1975).

Heidegger, M.: Being and time (Harper & Row, New York 1962).

Holton, G.: Thematic origins of scientific thought: Kepler to Einstein (Harvard University Press, Cambridge 1973).

Howard, R.J.: Three faces of hermeneutics (University of California Press, Berkeley 1982).

Hubbs-Tait, L.: Performance and competence as predictors of decalage in the formal operational period (Boston University, Boston, unpubl. 1981).

Inhelder, B.; Piaget, J.: De la logique de l'enfant à la logique de l'adolescent: essai sur la con-
    struction des structures opératoires formelles (Presses Universitaires de France, Paris
    1955).
Inhelder, B.; Piaget, J.: The growth of logical thinking from childhood to adolescence (Basic
    Books, New York 1958).
Inhelder, B.; Piaget, J.: The early growth of logic in the child: classification and seriation (Nor-
    ton, New York 1964).
Kail, R.; Bisanz, J.: Information processing and cognitive development; in Reese, Advances in
    child development and behavior, vol. 17 (Academic Press, New York 1982).
Kant, I.: Foundations of the metaphysics of morals (Bobbs-Merrill, Indianapolis 1959; original-
    ly published 1785).
Karmiloff-Smith, A.: Cross-domain generalities versus modularity: are they mutually exclusive?
    (Society for Research in Child Development Meeting, Toronto, unpubl. 1985).
Kelley, D.: The evidence of the senses (LSU Press, Baton Rouge, in press).
Kitchener, K.S.; Kitchener, R.F.: The development of natural rationality: can formal operations
    account for it? In Meacham, Santilli, Social development in youth: structure and content
    (Karger, Basel 1981).
Kitchener, R.F.: Changing conceptions of the philosophy of science and the foundations of
    developmental psychology; in Kuhn, Meacham, On the development of developmental
    psychology (Karger, Basel 1983).
Klahr, D.: Transition processes in cognitive development; in Sternberg, Mechanisms in cogni-
    tive development (Freeman, San Francisco 1984).
Kohlberg, L.: From is to ought: how to commit the naturalistic fallacy and get away with it in
    the study of moral development; in Mischel, Cognitive development and epistemology
    (Academic Press, New York 1971).
Koslowski, B.: The formal operational model of reasoning: limitations and alternatives (Jean
    Piaget Society, Philadelphia, unpubl. 1983).
Kramer, D.: Post-formal operations? A need for further conceptualization. Hum. Dev. 26:
    91–105 (1983).
Kuhn, D.: On the dual executive and its significance in the development of developmental psy-
    chology; in Kuhn, Meacham, On the development of developmental psychology (Karger,
    Basel 1983).
Kuhn, T.S.: The structure of scientific revolutions (University of Chicago Press, Chicago 1962).
Labouvie-Vief, G.: Beyond formal operations: uses and limits of pure logic in life-span develop-
    ment. Hum. Dev. 23: 141–161 (1980).
Labouvie-Vief, G.: Dynamic development and mature autonomy: a theoretical prologue. Hum.
    Dev. 25: 161–191 (1982).
Lakatos, I.: The methodology of scientific research programmes (Cambridge University Press,
    Cambridge 1978).
Laudan, L.: Progress and its problems: towards a theory of scientific growth (University of Cali-
    fornia Press, Berkeley 1977).
Leiser, D.: Piaget's logical formalism for formal operations: an interpretation in context. Dev.
    Rev. 2: 87–99 (1982).
Lunzer, E.A.: The development of formal reasoning: some recent experiments and their impli-
    cations; in Frey, Lang, Cognitive processes and science instruction (Huber, Bern 1973).
Lunzer, E.A.: Formal reasoning: a reappraisal; in Presseisen, Goldstein, Appel, Topics in cogni-
    tive development, vol. 2: Language and operational thought (Plenum Press, New York 1978).

MacIntyre, A.: After virtue (University of Notre Dame Press, Notre Dame 1981).

Mandler, J.M.: Representation; in Flavell, Markman, Handbook of child psychology, vol. 3: Cognitive development (Wiley, New York 1983).

Markman, E.M.: Empirical versus logical solutions to part-whole comparison problems concerning classes and collections. Child Dev. *49:* 168–177 (1978).

Markman, E.M.: Two different principles of conceptual organization; in Lamb, Brown, Advances in developmental psychology, vol. 1 (Erlbaum, Hillsdale 1981).

Markman, E.M.; Seibert, J.: Classes and collections: internal organization and resulting holistic properties. Cognitive Psychol. *8:* 561–577 (1976).

Markovits, H.: Awareness of the 'possible' as a mediator of formal thinking in conditional reasoning problems. Br. J. Psychol. *75:* 367–376 (1984).

Maturana, H.; Varela, F.: Autopoiesis and cognition (Reidel, Dordrecht 1980).

Meichenbaum, D.; Burland, S.; Gruson, L.; Cameron, R.: Metacognitive assessment; in Yussen, The growth of reflection in children (Academic Press, New York 1985).

Miller, L.K.; Barg, M.D.: Comparison of exclusive versus inclusive classes by young children. Child Dev. *53:* 560–567 (1982).

Minsky, M.; Papert, S.: Perceptrons (MIT, Cambridge 1969).

Moessinger, P.; Poulin-Dubois, D.: Piaget on abstraction. Hum. Dev. *24:* 347–353 (1981).

Moshman, D.: To *really* get ahead, get a metatheory; in Kuhn, Intellectual development beyond childhood (Jossey-Bass, San Francisco 1979).

Moshman, D.; Franks, B.A.: Development of the concept of inferential validity. Child Dev. (in press).

Moshman, D.; Timmons, M.: The construction of logical necessity. Hum. Dev. *25:* 309–323 (1982).

Murray, F.B.: The conservation paradigm: the conservation of conservation research; in Sigel, Brodzinsky, Golinkoff, New directions in Piagetian theory and practice (Erlbaum, Hillsdale 1981).

Neimark, E.D.: Current status of formal operations research. Hum. Dev. *22:* 60–67 (1979).

Nguyen-Xuan, A.; Lemaire, F.; Rousseau, J.: La sélection des informations dans la résolution du problème de série à trois termes. J. Psychol. norm. path. *71:* 297–317 (1974).

Nickles, T.: Introductory essay: scientific discovery and the future of philosophy of science; in Nickles, Scientific discovery, logic, and rationality (Reidel, Dordrecht 1980a).

Nickles, T.: Can scientific constraints be violated rationally? In Nickles, Scientific discovery, logic, and rationality (Reidel, Dordrecht 1980b).

Norton, D.L.: Personal destinies: a philosophy of ethical individualism (Princeton University Press, Princeton 1976).

O'Brien, D.; Overton, W.F.: Conditional reasoning following contradictory evidence: a developmental analysis. J. exp. Child Psychol. *30:* 44–61 (1980).

Overton, W.F.: World-views and their influence on psychological theory and research: Kuhn-Lakatos-Laudan; in Reese, Advances in child development and behavior, vol. 18 (Academic Press, New York 1984).

Overton, W.F.; Newman, J.L.: Cognitive development: a competence-activation/utilization approach; in Field, Houston, Quay, Troll, Finley, Review of human development (Wiley, New York 1982).

Overton, W.F.; Reese, H.W.: Conceptual prerequisites for an understanding of stability-change and continuity-discontinuity. Int. J. Behav. Dev. *4:* 99–123 (1981).

Palmer, S.E.: Fundamental aspects of cognitive representation; in Rosch, Lloyd, Cognition and categorization (Erlbaum, Hillsdale 1978).

Papert, S.: Mindstorms (Basic Books, New York 1980).

Pascual-Leone, J.: Constructive problems for constructive theories: the current relevance of Piaget's work and a critique of information-processing simulation psychology; in Kluwe, Spada, Developmental models of thinking (Academic Press, New York 1980).

Pascual-Leone, J.; Sparkman, E.: The dialectics of empiricism and rationalism: a last methodological reply to Trabasso. J. exp. Child Psychol. *29:* 88–101 (1980).

Pepper, S.C.: World hypotheses (University of California Press, Berkeley 1942).

Piaget, J.: Essai sur les transformations des opérations logiques (Presses Universitaires de France, Paris 1952).

Piaget, J.: The child's construction of reality (Basic Books, New York 1954).

Piaget, J.: Structuralism (Basic Books, New York 1970a).

Piaget, J.: Piaget's theory; in Mussen, Carmichael's manual of child psychology; 3rd ed. (Wiley, New York 1970b).

Piaget, J.: Biology and knowledge (University of Chicago Press, Chicago 1971).

Piaget, J.: Essai de logique opératoire; 2nd ed. (Dunod, Paris 1972a).

Piaget, J.: Intellectual evolution from adolescence to adulthood. Hum. Dev. *15:* 1–12 (1972b).

Piaget, J.: Understanding causality (Norton, New York 1974).

Piaget, J.: L'équilibration des structures cognitives: problème central du développement (Presses Universitaires de France, Paris 1975).

Piaget, J.: Le possible, l'impossible et le nécessaire. Archs Psychol. *44:* 281–299 (1976).

Piaget, J.: Recherches sur l'abstraction réfléchissante (Presses Universitaires de France, Paris 1977a).

Piaget, J.: Essai sur la nécessité. Archs Psychol. *45:* 235–251 (1977b)/Hum. Dev. *29* (1986).

Piaget, J.: Success and understanding (Harvard University Press, Cambridge 1978).

Piaget, J.: Recherches sur les correspondances (Presses Universitaires de France, Paris 1980a).

Piaget, J.: Les formes élémentaires de la dialectique (Gallimard, Paris 1980b).

Piaget, J.: Le possible et le nécessaire, vol. 1: L'évolution des possibles chez l'enfant (Presses Universitaires de France, Paris 1981).

Piaget, J.: Le possible et le nécessaire, vol. 2: L'évolution du nécessaire chez l'enfant (Presses Universitaires de France, Paris 1983).

Piaget, J.; Inhelder, B.: The origin of the idea of chance in children (Norton, New York 1975).

Piattelli-Palmarini, M.: How hard is the 'hard core' of a scientific program? In Piattelli-Palmarini, Language and learning: the debate between Jean Piaget and Noam Chomsky (Harvard University Press, Cambridge 1980).

Piéraut-LeBonniec, G.: The development of modal reasoning: genesis of necessity and possibility notions (Academic Press, New York 1980).

Piéraut-LeBonniec, G.; Rappe du Cher, E.: Le périmètre du carré: exemple de construction d'une coordination des significations. Archs Psychol. *50:* 285–301 (1982).

Popper, K.: Conjectures and refutations (Harper, New York 1965).

Potter, V.G.: Charles S. Peirce: on norms and ideals (University of Massachusetts Press, Worcester 1967).

Powell, P.M.: Stage 4a: category operations and interactive empathy; in Commons, Richards, Armon, Beyond formal operations: late adolescent and adult cognitive development (Praeger, New York 1984).

Author Index

Subject Index